PRAYERS FOR SUCCESS

Igniting the World to Achieve Success

Daily Prayers for Marketplace Influencers

JACQUI SHOWERS

JASSAI Publishing • Detroit, Michigan

PRAYERS FOR SUCCESS:
IGNITING THE WORLD TO ACHIEVE SUCCESS
Copyright © 2019 by Jacqui Showers
JASSAI Publishing, a Michigan Company

JASSAI Publishing
A Division of JASSAI LLC
P. O. Box 32909 • Detroit, MI 48232-0909

ISBN: 978-0-9897074-0-4

All rights reserved. No part of this publication may be reproduced, stored in a retrieval system, nor transmitted in any form or by any means—electronic, mechanical, photocopy, recording, nor any other—except for brief quotations in printed reviews, without the prior permission of the publisher, except as provided by the United States of America copyright law.

For special discounts on bulk purchases, please contact JASSAI Publishing at: prayersforsucccess@gmail.com.

Creative Consultant: Leon Holmes

Cover Design by JASSAI Publishing

Interior Layout: Selah Branding & Design LLC

Editing: Imani Kenyatte

Printed in the United States of America
[This title is also available as an e-book]

DEDICATION

To the memory of my beloved mother,
Rosie Showers, who trained me to embrace
and increase in my faith and relationship in God
through prayer, and always believed that I could
become whatever I endeavored to do.

To the memory of my sister, Portia Gentry,
who mentored me in my walk with Jesus Christ and
whose life of faith continues to inspire me to achieve
success in my faith walk.

To the memory of Patricia Holmes-Ellison,
my beloved sister and best friend forever,
who encouraged me to write
when I was too afraid to write.

To the millions of people around the world
who read *Prayers for Success* every day and have
been encouraged to achieve phenomenal success
as they become all God envisioned
so they can experience what God S.A.W.W.
(Spiritual Abundance Wholeness and Wealth).

PREFACE

Oftentimes, when God gives us an assignment, our first inclination is to say, "I can't do that." In the finiteness of who we are, we can't seem to fathom that God, in His infiniteness, knows what is inside of us. So, our answer echoes from the limitations of our existence in this world.

It was no different for me.

Before I could even embrace the assignment, I had already responded with a resounding, "I can't." As God does most times, He continued to impress upon me that I could, in fact, do what He had asked of me. Finally, I acquiesced to His request.

In 2011, I started writing daily prayers. Every week, I wrote *Showers' Blessing Inspirations*, and a prayer was always included. It was just hard for me to wrap my mind around writing a prayer every single day.

I knew this trepidation stemmed from years of not having confidence in my writing. Although I had worked vehemently for years to overcome it, every now and then, it tries to rear its ugly head. It was soon overpowered by my obedience to write a daily prayer. I learned how to conquer fear and all of its nuances by just doing it.

So I did.

When I wrote that first prayer, I knew it was for others. But I soon learned that this journey has been as much for me as it has been for those who read the prayers. Every prayer that is written comes from the depths of my soul to empower and exhort others to live the abundant life God envisioned for them. One of the most amazing things, to me, is when one of the prayers comes back to encourage me. Pinterest has been a constant reminder of the power of social media. I read every prayer that is re-pinned. In more instances than I can recall, the prayer which may have been written years, months or weeks ago, speaks to the very essence of my present position in any given moment. It is as though I experience the prayer for the first time. It speaks to me and encourages me.

It's amazing how one act of obedience can have far-reaching effects for others all around the world. I will never forget the day my niece told me she had to show me something. She grabbed her phone and searched through her Facebook posts.

Finally, she handed me her phone and said, "Your prayers are reaching a lot of people." She showed me how my prayers were in a private group on Facebook, in which she was a member. She knew the woman didn't know me and I didn't know her. When she saw my prayer she exclaimed, "That's Jacqui's prayer!"

Our mandate is to go into all of the world. Sometimes, we may not physically go there, but our talents and gifts can reach the world as we minister the gospel. These prayers are ministerial tools—not just for those in the household of faith—but for everyone. They are expressly written to move beyond the four walls of tradition into the wall-less-ness of the marketplace.

These marketplace prayers can be prayed quickly. They are definitely designed for the hustle-and-bustle of life we have come to know with the advent of the information and digital age.

FOREWORD

Joshua 1:8 says, *This Book of the Law shall not depart from your mouth, but you shall meditate in it day and night, that you may observe to do according to all that is written in it. For then you will make your way prosperous, and then you will have good success. (King James Version)*

The prayers contained in this book are a roadmap to help us put God first by meditating on His Word. As a result, we are guaranteed to have good success.

As a successful marketplace influencer herself, Jacqui Showers has gifted us all with a unique set of quick, yet powerful, prayers for the on-the-go professional. These prayers, birthed out of her spirit over several years, draw us closer to the heartbeat of God as He expands our spheres of influence and impact.

I have known Jacqui for nearly three decades, and I have personally witnessed her walk with the Lord. With each passing year, she continues to model Christ-like behavior in the marketplace. The Bible encourages us to let our light shine before men so they will see our good works and glorify God.

As you read the pages of this book, you, too, can discover how you can grow stronger in intimacy with God—for true success can only be found in Him.

Lori George Billingsley
Global Corporate Executive
and Marketplace Influencer

JANUARY

Prayer is what connects us to God, enabling us to fulfill our hopes, anticipations and expectations. There is a certain amount of hope, anticipation and expectation when a new year begins. People make all types of plans and resolutions as though bringing them to pass solely depends on their own abilities. There is a certain amount of truth to that notion. But for them to truly come to pass, one must commit them to God. God alone is the one who truly makes them happen.

PROVERBS 16:1, 3, 9

1 January

Father, As I stand on the threshold of a new year, there are things and situations that don't appear to have life. I can't seem to do anything to bring them back to life. I need a strategy and a Rhema Word that will breathe new life. I know beyond belief that when you pronounce life, the very essence of its existence is resurrected. Bless me not to give up, but to believe and speak with unwavering, steadfast faith, that renewed life and fervency has been breathed on them as they are resuscitated back to life. Because of this supernatural resuscitation, I know that ears haven't heard and eyes haven't seen the blessing and abundance I will experience in this year. Amen.

1 CORINTHIANS 2:9

January 2

Father, Enhance my instincts to not only discern opportunities, but to act on them. No longer will I draw back or be afraid to move forward. You said that when I knock, doors will open. I will move swiftly through those open doors of opportunity with diligence, excellence, confidence, integrity, discipline, enthusiasm and dedication. Wow! There is nothing but success awaiting me. Amen.

REVELATION 3:8

3 JANUARY

Father, You have entrusted me with a business. You have called me to exercise good stewardship over that business. I unequivocally understand that you are the true owner and I work for you. Everything I do, I will do in excellence as unto you. I will not be slothful in business, but fervently profitable. Daily, I will keep you apprised of every situation as you provide clear direction and guidance for optimum success. Amen.

ROMANS 12:11

January 4

Father, During this first month of t he year, I'm establishing healthy, productive habits that I want to maintain throughout the year. For me to do that, I need your guidance every step of the way. I need help—not just for this month—but each and every month of the year as you guide me down a path where I will experience good success every time. Amen.

JOSHUA 1:8-9

5 January

Father, I realize you have so much for me. Sometimes, I find myself not doing everything I need to do. But I know when I team up with you, success is always mine. Bless me to begin my day with you, seeking you throughout the day for your guidance and direction. When the day ends, remind me to spend more time thanking you for an awesomely successful day. Amen.

PROVERBS 3:5-12

January 6

Father, There is so much happening in the world. It seems as though you have been left out. Bless us to never forget you and to recognize you in all things because you are in all things. Amen.

PROVERBS 3:6

7 JANUARY

Father, There have been so many people who have lost their jobs. Those who have a job are overworked and often doing the jobs of two or three people. Touch the hearts of the leaders from every sphere of influence in our society, not to be so driven by money that they lose sight of their most precious commodity—human capital.

Bless them to honor and do the right thing by their employees, who make them successful every day. Bless them to treat their employees as they would want to be treated: with respect, commitment and loyalty. Amen.

EPHESIANS 6:6-9

January 8

Father, I'm working on this strategic plan and I need your guidance. Anoint my hands to write the words so whoever reads it can run purposefully with the vision. Bless each of us to adhere to the vision as we systematically achieve each goal with a spirit of excellence. Bless us to harmoniously work in unity as we experience unimaginable success. Amen.

HABAKKUK 2:1-2

9 JANUARY

Father, Sometimes it seems as though I have so much to do, yet not enough time to do it all. Teach me how to manage my time effectively so I can apply my heart to wisdom. Bless me to maximize each moment by establishing a daily schedule and diligently adhering to it in order to successfully complete each assignment every day. Amen.

PSALM 90:12

January 10

Father, Oftentimes, I find myself squandering away time. I need your strength to overcome those things that cause me to procrastinate. Yesterday, I said I would do it tomorrow. Yet, when tomorrow came, I did nothing. No longer will I put off tomorrow what I can do today. Procrastination is nothing but a thief, and it will no longer steal, kill and destroy my success or my future. Amen.

PROVERBS 6:4

11 JANUARY

Father, I exercise my body daily because it is the temple of the Holy Spirit. Bless me to take care of my body and bring it under subjection to your Word. My commitment to exercise and my desire to be in peak shape enables me to accomplish my assignment with passion, confidence and courage on my path to victory. Amen.

1 CORINTHIANS 6:19-20

January 12

Father, I eat to live, but I don't live to eat. I know that you have created the stomach for food and food for the stomach, but it was never your intention for food to control me. Bless me to establish healthy eating habits and not consume food that destroys my body, mind and ultimately, my soul. Bless me to make wise food choices that enable me to operate at peak performance. It is only then that I am able to conquer unhealthy eating habits and win at life every time. Amen.

1 Corinthians 6:12-13a

13 January

Father, You have placed me in this position for a reason. Regardless of how tough it may be, bless me to embrace the assignment with passion and give me the ability to perform with a spirit of excellence. I know you placed me in this position for your glory. When it is time for this assignment to end, I will be released. During this assignment, bless me to celebrate all that it entails in preparation for a higher level of responsibility, commitment and success. Amen.

PSALM 75:6-7

January 14

Father, Age is just a mere number and I will no longer be in bondage to it. Regardless of my age, I know you have impregnated me with so much potential that if I lived to be a thousand years old, I will never tap into the full reservoir of skills, talents and blessings you have for me. Regardless of my age, I will never stop dreaming and believing that you have created me for greatness. I will definitely achieve greatness in my lifetime. Amen.

Acts 10:34-35

15 January

Father, Retirement is not an option. There is so much more for me to do in creating a better world to live, work, play and worship in. I am a Kingdom solutionist, created to passionately solve problems until I have taken my last breath. When I do, I know I will have fulfilled my God-given assignment. As a creative force made in your image, the magnitude of my life will be experienced for many days, even beyond my existence in the earth. Amen.

PSALM 92:12-15

January 16

Father, Thank you for giving me dream seeds. I will not allow them to just lie dormant, unopened as mere images in the crevices of my mind. I will plant them and water them daily as they blossom into a beautiful bouquet of uncommon achievements and unparalleled success. Amen.

PSALM 126:4-6

17 JANUARY

Father, I'm so excited about the seeds of conception inside of me waiting to come forth. Although the journey has been long, I'm excited about the birthing of my dreams. You have been there every step of the way, guiding and directing me. When I wanted to give up, you were always there, encouraging me to push ahead. I thank you for everyone you sent to assist me in the process. I thank you for impregnating me with dream seeds of purpose that are bursting with new life all around me. Amen.

1 CHRONICLES 28:20-21

January 18

Father, I realize that there is so much for me. I will not be afraid to venture beyond my comfort zone. My boundaries are enlarged—not just my geographical boundaries, but the boundaries of my mind. Each day, you do exceedingly beyond my loftiest imagination. I unequivocally know I can have whatever you say I can have in this vast world of opportunities. Every single day, I revel in the abundant life you promised and envisioned for me. Amen.

John 10:10

19 January

Father, The rain drops of life may fall, but I will not be overwhelmed. I am an overcomer. I know that these are your showers of blessing raining down on me. They represent your promise that I am coming forth as pure gold. No matter what happens, I am already victorious in everything I do. The rain drops only proclaim that the manifestation of your best for me is yet to come. At the end of the rainbow, are your promises of an abundant life, chocked full of gold victories again and again and again. Amen.

Ezekiel 34:26-27

January 20

Father, Thank you for the mentors in my life
who encourage me and provide wise counsel.
I can never repay them for their time and effort.
Because you placed them in my life, I am better.
I am stronger. I show my ultimate appreciation
for their sacrifice to ensure my success by
encouraging and mentoring someone else
as they have done for me. Amen.

PROVERBS 27:17

21 January

Father, I thank you for your abundance of common sense, wisdom, business acumen and intelligence. They are more powerful than muscle or strength. Any enterprise that is built by wise planning becomes strong through common sense, and profits wonderfully by keeping abreast of the facts. Strategic planning and wise counsel are major weapons in my arsenal to achieve maximum success in every endeavor. Amen.

PROVERBS 2:6-8, 24:3-4

January 22

Father, Sometimes, I think that work wouldn't be so hard if the people weren't there. Then I realize that you have placed me in my position, especially in working with others, to be a bright light of faith, hope and love. Success is inherent in being able to effectively work with all people, regardless of their personalities. Bless me to be able to work with others and to celebrate the differences that make us one in achieving our goals. Amen.

MATTHEW 5:16

23 JANUARY

Father, I am so close to achieving all you have shown me. I am ready to move out of the realm of almost into the realm of achievement. I don't want to look back and regret that I was so close to victory—haunting words bellow out that I was almost successful. You created me to be successful, and I will be relentless in pursuit of the fulfillment of my dreams. I will not stop or allow anyone else to deter me from my dreams. Fear no longer has dominion over me and will not be a catalyst in preventing me from forging ahead with perseverance and determination. Sad words such as—"not quite," and "but almost" are no longer a part of my vernacular. "I can," "I will," and "I have already achieved" are words that propel me to victory every time. Amen.

PHILIPPIANS 3:13-14

January 24

Father, Today, I present my body as a living sacrifice, holy and acceptable to you. It is beyond a diet or mere words, but I am committed to establishing a healthy lifestyle. No longer will I consume unhealthy foods, overeat to the point of gluttony or remain sedentary. I take authority over my physical well-being. I will no longer be conformed to unhealthy habits, but I am transformed to experience an abundantly healthy lifestyle.
Amen.

ROMANS 12:1-2

25 January

Father, All of us have fallen short of your glory. Bless me to provide the same grace and mercy you have bestowed upon me onto others. Rather than pass harsh judgment, bless me to exhibit the same compassion toward others that you have exhibited toward me. Perfect love conquers all. Bless me to exhibit love to everyone, regardless if I personally know them or not. Bless me to love, even if people have done anything wrongful against me. You are love! I am made in your image; therefore I am a vessel of love, showering others with your love wherever I go. In doing so, you will be glorified at home, at worship and in the marketplace. Amen.

ROMANS 3:23

January 26

Father, I thank you for releasing me from the bondage of debt. It was like a trellis around my neck and I just couldn't break free from it. Regardless of how you set me free from debt, I learned some valuable lessons about exercising discipline in spending and managing my affairs with integrity. I know I made the vow, and I thank you for blessing me to honor the vow and pay my debt. Even though it may appear as though it was too much, you also made a way of escape for me to come from under the bondage of credit. In the midst of it, I am no longer slave to the master called credit. I have been set free by the blood of the Lamb and the words of my testimony.

Hallelujah! Thank you, God! Amen.

DEUTERONOMY 15:1-3

27 January

Father, In the transitioning of seasons, I celebrate all that I have learned as I move forward with confidence. Regardless of the trials and triumphs, every experience has brought me to this place of juxtaposition as I meander out of one season into the next. I rejoice in knowing that nothing but great things await me … the good, the bad and the indifferent. Each is a cornerstone in building my character to withstand the vicissitudes of life with confidence and courage. Amen.

Ecclesiastes 3:1, 11

January 28

Father, Nothing quenches my thirst like entering into communion with you at the break of dawn. Every morning, my heart longs and thirsts for more of you as I tear myself away to begin my day. There is no bitterness in my thirst because your water is as sweet as the honeycomb. I find solace in knowing that when the day breaks tomorrow, I will be there once again, consuming the life-sustaining water that only you can provide. Amen.

PSALM 42:1-2

29 January

Father, Regardless of the impossibility of the promise, I believe beyond belief that the promise will happen. I will not have doubts about the promise. I will not worry or be anxious about the promise. Every day, my faith and trust increase as I praise you even before the promise happens. I am completely persuaded that you are more than well able to fulfill the promise and I will experience great success. Amen.

Hebrews 10:23

January 30

Father, My employability is directly tied to my perceived perception of my usefulness and having confidence in my capabilities. I am well able to get the job done because I am forever learning innovative ideas to help any company succeed. Thank you for transforming my mindset to know my worth as a valuable asset in providing solutions for the employer who hires me.

Amen.

PHILIPPIANS 4:13

31 January

Father, You creatively carved out a path for my success that is inherent in the invisibility of my dreams becoming visible. Bless me to never give up because the plans you have for me are too numerous to count. Keep me from acting on my dreams prematurely. Enable me to be patient in the process as I team with you in making all my dreams a reality. Amen.

Jeremiah 29:11

FEBRUARY

Prayer transforms your mind
to know that God wants nothing
but great things for you. Every day
when you incorporate prayer into your
plans and your daily walk, you can't
help but experience great success.

JOSHUA 1:9

1 FEBRUARY

Father, The entrepreneurial spirit inside of me is awakened. Bless me with the ideal business that you have envisioned for me. Give me the discernment to operate within your timing to ensure the success of the business. Bless me with wisdom, understanding, counsel, might and knowledge to manage the business with integrity and confidence. Furthermore, give me strategic alliances to mentor me through the process. Amen.

PROVERBS 19:20-21

February 2

Father, Oh, what a great day it is! This day is chock-full of nothing but success! Every minute has success written on it. Every encounter is successful! Every project is successful! Every meeting is successful! Every phone call is successful! Every text message is successful! Every tweet is successful! Every posting is successful! I am rejoicing in this day because you created it for my success. Oh, what a great day it is, because I am successful in everything that I do! Amen.

PSALM 118:23-24

3 FEBRUARY

Father, I need you to reveal the things that have kept me from succeeding. I am no longer afraid to confront them. In confronting them, I overcome them. I overcome daily by the blood of the Lamb and the words of my testimony. Acknowledgement of these obstacles enables me to overcome them. They no longer master me, but I master them. I am an overcomer! I am a conqueror! I am a winner! Amen.

REVELATION 12:11

February 4

Father, You have made a way of escape for me. As you strengthen me each day with supernatural endurance, I will mount up with wings like an eagle. I will run this race and I will not be weary. I will walk and I will not faint. I will never give up! I will never cave in! I will never stop because I am relentless to achieve all you envisioned for me. I am a formidable force, anointed with your supernatural strength to endure as I reach the high mark of your calling for unparalleled success. Amen.

Isaiah 40:31

5 February

Father, I have traveled around this mountain long enough. I am getting off this treadmill where I have been going nowhere fast. I run this race with one intention, and that is to be successful. Success is an inherent part of who you created me to be. The only way I can do that is by doing the things I may not want to do every day. I am on a new path. It has some speed bumps, but I am unstoppable and I will succeed. Amen.

DEUTERONOMY 2:3

February 6

Father, Thank you for a love affair that is totally beyond compare. Nothing compares to my relationship with you. Your love is endless. Your love is nonjudgmental. Your love is unconditional. I give you the same love you give me, and I give that same love to others as well. Amen.

ROMANS 8:38-39

7 FEBRUARY

Father, It is time for me to put the oxygen mask on myself. For me to be effective, I have to use wisdom and take care of my own well-being before I can assist others. Strengthen me as I build myself up so I can make an indelible impact as a marketplace influencer. Amen.

1 TIMOTHY 4:15-16

FEBRUARY 8

Father, How in the world do I expect to succeed if I won't take time to plan? I may not like it, but planning is critical to be successful. No longer will fear prevent me from planning. Procrastination does not have any place in my life. It no longer conquers me, but I conquer it. I am more than a conqueror because I maximize every minute of every day, and that begins with planning. I am a planner; therefore, I am a winner. Amen.

PROVERBS 24:27

9 FEBRUARY

Father, The vision you gave me, propels me to be successful in everything I do. I am running full-speed ahead with the vision. I have written and shared the vision. Your favor on the vision is the catalyst that enables others to not just embrace the vision, but to run with it. Nothing can stop the vision's success. You are the forerunner who places favor in the hearts of every philanthropist, customer, client and funder to ensure we have the revenue and resources needed for the vision to succeed. Amen.

HABAKKUK 2:2

February 10

Father, I am no longer going to allow
my past to prevent me from forging forward.
It's called "the past" because it has passed.
I will only take from it what is beneficial.
Everything else, I will forget and press toward
the mark of your high calling. I have my sight
set on winning. I am not in a race of futility,
but I am in this race to win every time!
Amen.

PHILIPPIANS 3:13-14

11 FEBRUARY

Father, Bless me to be a leader who motivates, not one who misleads or exploits; a leader who knows my business is your business and who promotes honesty in the marketplace; a leader who abhors wrongdoing, and provides morally sound equitable leadership; a leader who welcomes truth and is not afraid to receive wise counsel from godly advisors. Help me to be well-balanced in my temperament, as I invigorate others to perform to their highest potential.

Amen.

PROVERBS 16:10-15

February 12

Father, I walk by faith and not by sight. Faith is the substance of things hoped for and the evidence of things not seen. Although I cannot see it, my now-faith with lots of action propels me to unimaginable success. Amen.

Hebrews 11:1

13 FEBRUARY

Father, You are not bankrupt. If you're not bankrupt, neither am I. Fill me the more with your love, your strength, your joy, your peace, your wealth, your wisdom, your understanding, your counsel, your might, your knowledge.

Fill me with more and more of you.

Amen.

EPHESIANS 3:16-19

February 14

Father, I am not physically bankrupt.
I am not spiritually bankrupt. I am not
financially bankrupt. Wealth and riches are in
my house and I dwell in the overflow of your
abundant prosperity and blessings in every
area of my life. Amen.

Psalm 112:1-3

15 February

Father, Things may look bleak, but that is deception. I don't look at things as they are. I speak into existence those things that are not, and they will be. My faith is sightless, because I know that all things are working together for my good. You are providing all my needs according to your riches in glory through Christ Jesus. Therefore, I call forth supernatural provisions from the royal treasures. I have that authority because I have brought all my tithes and offerings into the storehouse and you are pouring out a blessing too massive for me to receive and rebuking my devourers. I will not be ashamed because of your showers of blessing. It is an endless blessing that keeps on giving again and again and again. Amen.

Job 22:28

February 16

Father, I woke up this morning with love in my heart. Teach me to love as your Son loved—to love my foes as I love my friends. I am a well-spring of love, showering others with unconditional love. When everything else fades, the only thing that shall remain is love. Love is the strongest force—it is stronger than death. Love is a mighty weapon, and perfect love casts out all fear. Love is what propels me to succeed. When I succeed, I lead others to success. Loving to help others is a reflection of you. Amen.

MATTHEW 22:39

17 FEBRUARY

Father, My position of increase has shifted for my good. I am not the tail—I am the head. I am not beneath—I am above. I am no longer enslaved to lenders—I am the lender! I no longer operate below the bar because I operate exponentially above the bar! I set the parameters for my success because you are doing exceedingly, abundantly, above all I could ever ask or think because of the intensity of the power that dwells inside of me. I can't help but be at the top of my game every day because I am part of a winning team—a team with you, the Son and the Holy Spirit. Amen.

DEUTERONOMY 28:12-13

FEBRUARY 18

Father, I am bursting forth with new life, new ideas, witty inventions and new opportunities! Daily, you bless me with vision, strategies and tactical maneuvers to be successful. Everything I need is already inside of me. It's just waiting to burst forth. When I feel I don't quite understand, I go to the Holy Spirit, my built-in, all-knowing computer, who provides me with all wisdom, understanding, counsel, strength and knowledge needed to be successful. The Holy Spirit's memory bank never crashes because it connects me to the illimitable power of you and the Son. Amen.

ISAIAH 11:2-3

19 FEBRUARY

Father, It may be a jungle out here, but I am a conqueror of the jungle. I am a descendant of the Lion of Judah! I praise you when I'm down! I praise you when I'm up! I praise you all the time! My praise enables me to conquer the attacks in the jungle every time. When my praises go up in full force, your blessings come down even more forceful, guaranteeing that I am victorious in everything that I do! Amen.

2 CHRONICLES 20:22

February 20

Father, Thank you for waking me up this morning with excitement for a brand new day. How awesome is today! It is as awesome as I make it! I will make it an awesome day, as I maximize your awesome gift of time augmented with my vast skills and abilities to succeed. I will not squander them. I will use them while it is such an awesome day. I will achieve awesome success in everything I do! This is the day which the Lord hath made; I will rejoice and be glad in it. Amen.

PSALM 118:24

21 FEBRUARY

Father, I dream big! I think big! I expect big things! I take big actions! You are a big God, so all I can do is function in the bigness of who you are. That means nothing but big, monumental success is coming my way! Amen.

EPHESIANS 3:20

February 22

Father, Everything I ask you for, I receive.
Everything I seek, I find. Every door I knock
on, opens. I am not afraid to ask because I have
already received everything you have for me.
I am not afraid to seek because I have already
found the abundance of blessings you have for me.
I am not afraid to knock on any size door.
The doors of opportunity have been
flung open, and I confidently walk through
them with courage. Amen.

MATTHEW 7:7-8

23 FEBRUARY

Father, Life is absolutely wonderful! I wake up with renewed vigor every day. I know that nothing but success is mine! Doors of opportunity are opening like never before. Absolutely no man can shut them. I have peace that surpasses human comprehension, with every door you shut because I know you have a better one for me. I walk confidently and courageously through those open doors because you have already equipped me with every skill and talent needed to succeed. I will never cast away my confidence because the rewards are manifold. Life is absolutely wonderful, and I am living life to its fullest as I walk through door, after door, after door of opportunity on my pathway to stupendous success! Amen.

Lamentations 3:22-24

February 24

Father, I am impassioned and emboldened
to be the best me I can be. I can't be anyone else,
and I don't want to be anybody but me. All
of the blessings you have for me are for me.
All the success you have for me is for me.
If I am trying to be somebody else, I will miss
all that you have for me. I have no intentions
of missing you! Amen.

PSALM 139:13-15

25 February

Father, I am fearless and I am free! Evil tidings will not prevent me from passionately pursuing my dreams that you have placed inside of me with passion. I am unstoppable and I will accomplish the impossible because you are the God of impossibility. I have teamed up with you, which ensures that everything I do will prosper beyond my wildest imaginations. Amen.

Mark 10:27

FEBRUARY 26

Father, When I woke up this morning, I was so glad to be me! You have fearfully and wonderfully created me for greatness. Each day, your mercies are new every morning and you load me with too many benefits to number. You have gifted me with so many talents, that I can't help but succeed at everything I do. Amen.

PSALM 68:19

27 February

Father, Thank you for the opportunity to provide oversight for this business. Bless me to exercise the utmost integrity in providing compassionate and bold leadership. Give me insight on how to expand, grow and develop the business. Enlarge my territory by providing the wisdom, knowledge, understanding, counsel and might that I need to succeed. Let me never forget that it is you who has given me the power to amass wealth, and not by my efforts alone. Amen.

PROVERBS 4:25-27

February 28

Father, I will not be so caught up in perfection that I lose sight of excellence. Excellence is a spirit of faith inherent in what I do. Perfection is a spirit of fear that causes me to get caught up in the inertia of doing, to the point of never finishing. I operate in a spirit of excellence that is driven by great faith. That means that I will not get caught up in the inertia of perfection. I am driven by the spirit of excellence, which propels me forward to achieve the impossible. Amen.

Daniel 6:3

29 February

Father, Bless me to achieve my sales goals as I exercise the utmost skill, talent and integrity in bringing value to the marketplace. Increase my faith to know that every seed planted will increase.

For every phone call, email and meeting, the response will be favorable and lead to a positive outcome. Bless me not to become weary when the outcome I seek may not be the one I receive. Bless me to continue my journey with enthusiasm and a determination to not only succeed, but to represent you with excellence in the marketplace.

Amen.

COLOSSIANS 3:23-24

MARCH

Prayer enables you to know that there is nothing God will withhold from you, when you put Him first. His plans have always been for you to be successful beyond your wildest imaginations. God created you for success and He expects you to be successful. Even more than that, God wants you to be successful.

JEREMIAH 29:11

1 March

Father, All is well with me. I look to the cross for inspiration and courage. I may not always understand the crosses I must bear, but I do understand that the One who entrusted me with the cross also made a way of escape for me to endure with patience and joy. You poured your love in me through the Holy Spirit. I will never be ashamed by the beasts of this world. Through all you have entrusted me with, I overcome by the shed blood of the Lamb and the words of my testimony. Amen.

1 CORINTHIANS 10:13

March 2

Father, The death of the tomb will never stop my dreams from becoming a reality. Because of the shed blood, death and resurrection of Jesus, life springs forth on every idea and witty invention you placed inside of me. Those things that appear to be dead, lie in a living tomb, awaiting resurrection. I believe they will be resurrected with new life, new birth and new fervency. I will have a renewed passion in achieving every one of them. Amen.

MATTHEW 28:2

3 March

Father, You created life, so I could live it with abundance. You are an abundant God. As your child, I dwell in the abundance of my Father. There is no good thing that you will withhold from me as I walk uprightly with you. Amen.

PSALM 84:11

March 4

Father, Words pour out of my mouth with power and authority. Bless me to use these words as streams of increase in every aspect of my life. Every word that flows out of my mouth is a word of life, not death. In taking authority over my words, I create a world of abundance, once invisible, that is now manifested in the visible realm. Amen.

PROVERBS 18:21

5 MARCH

Father, The tides are turning. There are blue skies ahead. There are sunny days ahead. Yes, there are storms ahead. Regardless of the blue skies, the sunny days or the storms, I am victorious. You have fortified me to weather the vicissitudes of life with courage, confidence, faith and passion. Amen.

MATTHEW 8:23-26

MARCH 6

Father, What an awesome day just to behold the beauty of your masterpieces of miracles—human beings. You created not only me, but others so that we can be an encouragement to each other. You placed inside of us, the capacity to love as you love…to celebrate each other as you celebrate us. Bless me to celebrate all that makes us one and all that makes us different. Amen.

HEBREWS 3:13

7 MARCH

Father, I feel the breath of a new beginning, the breath that is breathing new life into me. The old has passed away and behold, I sense you are doing a new thing. It is springing forth with vigor and passion as I embrace yet another season of unparalleled success. A new beginning chocked full of the wonderment of the unknown awaits me. I'm excited to embrace all that it has in store for me. Amen.

ISAIAH 43:18-19

March 8

Father, I may not always understand the shifting of the seasons, but I am not afraid of the shift. New beginnings resonate in seasonal transitions on destiny's journey. I celebrate these transitions from one season to the next because you have fortified me for the journey. I embrace every opportunity as I confidently proceed down the path of success during the shifting of the season. Amen.

ECCLESIASTES 3:1, 11

9 MARCH

Father, I instinctively know there is a shifting taking place. Although doors may appear to be closed, I can see the beckoning light from the one door that remains ajar. Guide me to that door and give me the confidence, courage and boldness to walk through it. I look forward to leaving one season behind and walking into another season of bountiful opportunities.
Amen.

REVELATION 3:8

March 10

Father, There is a spring in my step.
There is a song on my lips. There is a book
at my fingertips. There is praise in my heart.
Today, I will spring forth as the bud of
creativity blossoms into a bouquet of
beautiful achievements. Amen.

Isaiah 35:1-2

11 MARCH

Father, Everywhere I look, there is so much joy. I have tapped into the wellspring of your oil of joy that strengthens me throughout the vicissitudes of life. No matter what comes my way, I know you have strengthened me to not only endure, but to excel. Amen.

COLOSSIANS 1:12

March 12

Father, I love my spouse and my children.
I thank you for your infinite wisdom to place
us together as a family. For me and my house,
we will serve you with all our hearts, minds,
strength and soul. We are knitted together by love.
It is this love that permeates the atmosphere
of our home for all to experience when they walk
through those doors. It is this love that cements
us together as a healthy, thriving
prosperous family. Amen.

JOSHUA 24:15

13 MARCH

Father, I thank you for the unity of my
family. I come against anything that tries to
separate us. We are strengthened daily by your
love. There is nothing that we cannot accomplish
together as a family. Bless us to work together,
play together and, most importantly, to pray
together. When we do this, we stay together.
United, we are a formidable force
to be reckoned with. Amen.

PSALM 133

March 14

Father, I refuse to be a spectator in life. I shall live life to its fullest. I will passionately pursue my goals and dreams with enthusiasm and excitement. No matter what, I will not allow anything to take me off my game. The course has been set, opportunities for success loom before me and, with each step, I am running this race—not to lose, but to win every time. Amen.

1 CORINTHIANS 9:24

15 March

Father, Everything I set my mind to do,
I am more than successful when I complete it.
I am fearless and free to accomplish every
endeavor with diligence, excellence, confidence,
integrity, discipline, enthusiasm and dedication.
I am no longer confused or scared about the
things that once confused me. You have given
me wisdom, understanding, counsel, might and
knowledge to do the impossible. The fear that
clouded my vision no longer exists. I can see
everything clearly and I move confidently
toward achieving the success you
envisioned for me. Amen.

2 Timothy 1:7

March 16

Father, Your favor places me in the presence of those of influence. I know it is because of your favor that doors are flinging open that no man can shut. I am prospering beyond measure in every aspect of my life. Because of your favor, every obstacle that has been a hindrance has been permanently removed. Those who are against me, have become the footstools that elevate me to success. Amen.

PSALM 110:1

17 MARCH

Father, You said give, and it shall be given back to me, good measure, pressed down, shaken together and running over shall men give unto me. I am a cheerful giver and find joy in giving. I thank you for blessing me with the ability to get wealth so that I can sow into the Kingdom and help others. All of my financial needs are met. Amen.

LUKE 6:38

March 18

Father, Thank you for providing me with insight on how to wisely invest. I know that it is your will for me to prosper and I thank you for providing me with wisdom as you reveal wealth-generating endeavors. I open my ears and eyes to hear your wise counsel. Thank you for orchestrating divine connections with trustworthy counselors to provide advice for sound investment practices. As I increase in wealth, I will never forget that you have given me the power to get wealth. For that, I am forever thankful. Amen.

DEUTERONOMY 8:18

19 MARCH

Father, Thank you for your financial wisdom. You have given me the power to get wealth and I exercise that power daily. I manage my affairs with integrity. You are providing for all my needs and there is nothing lacking in my life. Everything that I set my hands to do prospers because your favor and blessings are already on it. I excel in all that I do. Amen.

PSALM 90:17

March 20

Father, I am always grateful to you for just being you. Because you are you, I am the apple of your eye and I am always on your mind. I can't help but be optimistic when I wake up each day. Every day, you have something new for me. I embrace each day with a renewed vigor to soar beyond the stars. Amen.

Psalm 17:8

21 March

Father, The earth and everything in it is yours. You alone created the heavens and the earth, but you have given humankind a mandate as co-creators to build a civilization and infrastructure as we increase, multiply, subdue and take dominion in glorifying you. Bless me daily to walk out this mandate in transforming culture and having a tangible impact every day as a marketplace influencer. Amen.

Genesis 1:28

March 22

Father, You blessed me with such an awesome life. You gave me the instructions to live it to the fullest. Every day, I will live life to its abundance with unbridled enthusiasm. Daily, when I wake, all I can do is thank you for providing me with the skills and talents for success. I am so successful. My success is from the inside out. It is inside of me, but it is beyond me. It is what propels me to achieve unfathomable success in everything I do. You created this world with me in mind. You created this world for me to become the success you envisioned. For that, I am thankful. For that, I am grateful. For that, I will become all you envisioned in glorifying you in all I do. Amen.

EPHESIANS 2:10

23 MARCH

Father, Bless me to be as content in the blind spots of life as I am when I can see everything clearly. It is in the blind spots where my trust and faith increase exponentially. Although I may not be able to see all you have envisioned, I implicitly trust you in guiding me through the blind spots on my way to experience tremendous success, wealth and prosperity.
Amen.

JOB 11:7

March 24

Father, I may not completely understand everything that I need to do, but I know that you are my complete source of information. I ask you to anoint me with your wisdom, understanding, counsel, might and knowledg so I can excel at every endeavor. Because of this, I know I will be successful. Amen.

Isaiah 11:2

25 March

Father, You have given me the wisdom and power to get wealth. I will never think that I obtained this wealth through my own might. I know that it is because of your enabling Spirit. I thank you for giving me the strength to produce all this wealth as a confirmation of your covenant and promise. Amen.

DEUTERONOMY 8:17-18

March 26

Father, Thank you for your wisdom, which energizes me to excel and discover new innovative ways to provide solutions to others. As a Kingdom solutionist, I know that there is nothing I can't accomplish. You have anointed me with wisdom, understanding, counsel, might and knowledge to do the impossible. Amen.

Isaiah 11:2

27 MARCH

Father, Thank you for double defense—wisdom and money. Coupled together, these two defenses enable me to succeed like never before. I fully understand that money doesn't provide me wisdom; without wisdom, money will seep through my hands because of my lack of knowledge in managing it properly.

Money coupled with wisdom is double protection and fortifies me to succeed. Because I have both defenses complementing each other, I am unstoppable. I am able to succeed, and I have more than enough money in providing philanthropic solutions in the marketplace. Amen.

ECCLESIASTES 7:11

March 28

Father, I gaze in the mirror and I see what you see—I am spiritually, abundantly, wealthy and whole. You have placed so much inside of me. It has always been there, waiting for me to tap into the innate reservoir of resources to succeed. The plans you have for me are for an abundant future, paved with unparalleled success. You placed all of this inside of me when you knitted me together while I was yet in my mother's womb. Now the image I see is what you see—a spiritually, abundantly, wealthy and whole person. I'm so excited because now I truly know that my wealth is inherent in who you created me to be. Amen.

PSALM 139:14-18

29 MARCH

Father, I'm so excited! I overcome every discriminatory act that tries to prevent me from succeeding. My mind is transformed from the limitations irrational bigotry has tried to impose on me. You are a big God! You are an exceeding God! I have already overcome prejudice, discrimination and bigotry. My sights are set on succeeding because I envision myself as only you envision me. I know you have positioned me to be a success in everything I do. Amen.

ROMANS 8:31

March 30

Father, Who in the world said my age has anything to do with my success? I thank you for not being a respecter of persons. Regardless of my age, I succeed. You have impregnated me with skills, talents and dreams. I will achieve them all! I will soar against all odds. I nullify every negative word that claims I will not be successful. I refute every notion that says people will not hire me because of my age. Every age discrimination obstacle is brought down. I know that I am full of wisdom, understanding, counsel, might and knowledge to excel. I have the energy and stamina to succeed. Amen.

ROMANS 8:31

31 March

Father, I am so excited! I thank you for Jesus and His resurrection. He unselfishly took on the sins of this world, in order for me to be set free from bondage. I will not squander this freedom. With passion and fervency, I will fulfill the mandate to go into the entire world as my beautiful feet carry the Gospel to all men and women across the globe. Amen.

Romans 10:15

APRIL

Prayer opens doors to receive the
blessings of God. The reverberating
effects of God's blessings catapult you
from a poverty mentality and existence to
experience spiritual abundance, wholeness
and wealth in every area of your life.

PROVERBS 10:22

1 April

Father, A fool says in their heart that there is no God. I pray for all of those who have not come to the full knowledge of your existence. I pray that their eyes and hearts are open to receive the veracity of who you are and they will come into an intimate relationship with you. Amen.

PSALM 14:1

April 2

Father, When I think about how blessed I am,
I become overwhelmed with emotion.
Oh, your blessings are precious and
encompass me with so much joy and peace.
I am just ecstatic that in your infinite wisdom,
you chose me to be a blessing to others. Amen.

MATTHEW 5:16

3 April

Father, It gives me such joy to be a
blessing to others. Every time you bless me,
I, in turn, bless someone else. It is such a blessing
to be a blessing and brighten someone's life,
as you have done for me. Amen.

Luke 6:38

April 4

Father, What more can I say? The love you have for me is exemplified in the abundance of blessings you shower down on me. Your blessings have flung open doors of opportunities that I only once dreamed about. Now I'm living my dreams, blessing after blessing after blessing. Amen.

Ezekiel 34:26

5 April

Father, I can wait on the blessing as I meander through the process to its manifestation. Because of your blessings, I am increasing in patience, character and hope. The person who started the journey is not the person who will finish it. I will not only be ready to receive the blessing, I will also be able to manage the blessing. Thank you for trusting me with the blessing. Amen.

Isaiah 30:18

April 6

Father, I may never understand the twists and turns of life. But I do know that regardless of the twists and turns, every day, all things are working out for my good according to your purpose. Because they are being worked out for my good, I expect to succeed every time, every single day. Amen.

ROMANS 8:28

7 April

Father, Your blessing enables me to overcome every obstacle. I am no longer afraid of the obstacle courses of life because I know that on my way to receiving the blessing, I may have to go through some things. But I am reassured that I am blessed in the midst of it all and even more so on the other side of the obstacle course. Amen.

Deuteronomy 28:1-2

April 8

Father, Your favor is inherent in the blessing. You have placed favor on my hands and everything that I do is blessed. I work heartily unto you because your blessing on my diligent hands makes me rich and adds no sorrow to it. Amen.

Psalm 90:16-17
Proverbs 10:22 Proverbs 10:4

9 April

Father, Your blessings cause my mind to be transformed and renewed. I am no longer conformed to a limited mindset. I know you are doing exceedingly, abundantly, above all I could ever ask or think. I am experiencing great success because my powerful, positive thoughts create a world of illimitable possibilities. Amen.

Romans 12:2
Ephesians 3:20

April 10

Father, Your blessings make me rich and add no sorrow. You have not given me a spirit of fear, but of power, love and a sound mind. I will be anxious for nothing. I will not worry or fret because you are providing for all of my needs, even before I know what my needs are. I am not concerned about tomorrow because you have already made provisions for tomorrow.

You are my source and my resource.

For that, I am thankful. Amen.

PROVERBS 10:22

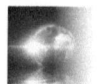

11 April

Father, I am not afraid of the terror
by night or the stalking pestilence that
lurks in the darkness. I am no longer
tormented by horrifying dreams or thoughts.
When I lay my head down, my sleep
will be sweet. I will wake up refreshed
and renewed. I decree that I shall live
and not die. I will declare your works
throughout the land. Amen.

PSALM 92:3

PSALM 3:24 PSALM 118:17

April 12

Father, Your blessings ensure that I experience divine health and healing every day. I have been redeemed from the curse of sickness and disease. Because of your blessings and the blood of Jesus, I bind the strongholds of sickness and disease. I loose myself from its grip that tries to prevent me from obtaining divine health and healing. I vociferously exclaim, "I am already healed by the stripes of Jesus Christ! I overcome by the blood of the Lamb and the words of my testimony. I am prosperous and in good health, even as my soul prospers. Amen.

GALATIANS 3:13 ISAIAH 53:5
REVELATIONS 12:11 3 JOHN 1:2

13 April

Father, No longer will I allow outside stimulus to prevent me from doing what I know I need to do. I am a trailblazer. I am a trendsetter. I will move circumspectly in blazing forward. Others gain courage to walk boldly into unfamiliar territory when I walk into unfamiliar territory. Bless me to move beyond myself so others can move beyond themselves. Amen.

Joshua 1:3

April 14

Father, Sometimes the mountain is a little steep and appears too hard to climb. But I know that I am going to make it. I may not know the future, but I do know the One who holds my future in His hands. Trusting and believing in You is more than enough assurance that I have already achieved success. Amen.

PSALM 31:15

15 APRIL

Father, Bless my expectations, words and prayers to be in symmetry with your Word. Out of the heart, the mouth speaks. Bless me to be mindful of every idle word spoken, as I expect you to do exceedingly, abundantly, above all that I could ever ask or think according to the power working inside of me. Amen.

MATTHEW 12:36
LUKE 6:45 EPHESIANS 3:20

APRIL 16

Father, Thank you for the thousand-fold blessing of wisdom, understanding, counsel, might and knowledge. I am a problem-solver because of your limitless blessing. There is nothing I can't do. I can do all things through Christ, who provides me with the fortitude to fulfill the assignment. Everything that I do increases a thousand times more! Amen.

ISAIAH 11:2

DEUTERONOMY 1:11 PHILIPPIANS 4:13

17 APRIL

Father, Your blessings far exceed natural boundaries. I am not limited by any barriers, but I invest in numerous diverse ventures all over the world that bring forth a bountiful return on my investment. I will not be slothful in business, but I will work fervently. My diligent hands make me rich, and I experience good success with every venture. Amen.

ECCLESIASTES 11:1-2
PROVERBS 10:4 ROMANS 12:11

April 18

Father, Thank you for the heir-ship of my blood-bought covenant right to the blessing. I am a chosen vessel. The thoughts you have for me number more than all the sand on the earth. These countless thoughts are for me to have a bright future, hope and an expected end. You created me to succeed. I am your masterful creation of success. Amen.

PSALM 139:17-18
JEREMIAH 29:11

19 April

Father, There is no way I will turn away from you! The road has been rough and the mountains may have been a little steep. I am too close to the unleashing of my blessing to turn back now. I will never ever give up! Amen.

James 1:12

April 20

Father, I hold fast to my profession of faith because I know that you are faithful to perform all that you have promised. Never will your word return to you empty. Every assigned Word from your promises will accomplish what it has been targeted to do. Your Word slashes every negative word that has been sent forth to prevent my blessings from flowing freely. Thank you, God, that your blessings are overtaking me! Amen.

HEBREWS 10:23

ISAIAH 55:11

21 April

Father, I thank you for being a God of covenant and a God of promise. If you said it, you will do it. If you spoke it, it has already taken place. I walk in the right-now blessing of your promises. My now faith is explosive as it ignites every blessing that you have for me to succeed. Amen.

Hebrews 11:1
Psalm 105:8 Numbers 23:19

April 22

Father, Oh that you would bless me, and bless me indeed! You are enlarging my territory across geographical borders and mental barriers. Every wall that tries to prevent me from moving forward to reap the benefits of my blessing, is being brought down. Every spirit of fear is being brought down as I hold fast to my confidence. I know it contains awesome rewards. Amen.

1 CHRONICLES 4:10

HEBREWS 10:35

23 April

Father, The freshness in the air resonates with the blossoming of new ideas and opportunities. I confidently move toward the new things overflowing with illimitable possibilities. My mind is flooded with witty, revenue-generating ideas and strategies. Every purposeful tactical strategy causes everything I do to prosper. I have good success. Amen.

JOSHUA 1:8 PROVERBS 8:12

April 24

Father, I am more than just a thinker, a wisher or a dreamer. I am a doer. As a doer who takes action, your blessing and favor are on everything I do. Every productive action I take is already blessed, simply because I migrated from dysfunction to function. Functioning at optimum performance assures me that I am walking in the abundance of your blessing every single day. Amen.

JAMES 1:22

25 April

Father, I will not let go of you until you bless me. If it means that I wrestle all night for this blessing, I will do it! I am relentless! I am determined that nothing will prevent me from receiving the abundance of blessing that you have for me. It is in the abundance of your blessing that I progressively and exponentially move from the lower rungs of the economic strata to millionaire status. I will make a difference in the earth. Amen.

GENESIS 32:24-26

April 26

Father, I am overtaken by your blessing. Although it may appear as though I don't have room enough to receive it, I receive all of it, even to the point of overflowing. You shower me daily with a blessing full of revenue-generating, intellectual properties. The beasts of this world will never cause me to be ashamed again because of the love you pour inside of me through Your Holy Spirit. I know you are doing exceedingly, abundantly, more than I could ever ask for or envision. Amen.

MALACHI 3:10-11

EZEKIEL 34:26 EPHESIANS 3:20

27 April

Father, I thank you for a chance encounter. Although it may appear to be a chance encounter, I know that it has been divinely orchestrated by you. This purposeful chance encounter is a blessing that you arranged for my destiny pathway to success. Thank you, God, for raining down yet another overflowing blessing full of unlimited opportunities. Amen.

Amos 3:3

April 28

Father, Thank you that an idea,
a witty invention, or a chance encounter
is the blessing that catapults me from the
poverty line to millionaire status. It is a blessing
that overflows with one opportunity
after another. It springs forth and
I can perceive it. If I can perceive it,
I believe beyond the point of knowing
I will more than achieve it. Amen.

PROVERBS 8:12

ISAIAH 43:19

29 April

Father, Daily, I am determined to succeed. It doesn't matter what happened yesterday. That's a done deal! I can't retrieve it so I can't allow it to prevent me from succeeding today. Tomorrow hasn't come yet and I will not fret about what may happen tomorrow. I only have today. Every day, I will wake up with the same determination. Today, I will seize the moment! Today, I will maximize my efforts! Today, I will be determined! Today, I will succeed! Amen.

MATTHEW 6:33-34

April 30

Father, I will do more than just live my dreams;
I will take ownership of them. I will do whatever
is necessary for my dreams to become reality.
I am committed to giving my energy, time, money,
sweat and tears each and every day to my dreams.
I will not be enslaved to someone else's dream.
I am in passionate pursuit of not just owning my
dreams, but making them a reality. Amen.

NUMBERS 12:6

PSALM 14:6 EPHESIANS 3:20

MAY

Praying every day moves
you beyond yourself to embrace
the mandate on your life.
This enables you to become
a blessing to others as
God continually blesses you.

Luke 6:38

2 Corinthians 9:10-11

May 1

Father, You bless me with such cheerfulness and, in turn, I will bless others with the same cheerfulness and generosity. Your constant overflowing kindness provides me with everything I need, so I am able to give even more freely to others. Thank you for blessing me to be a cheerful giver and a blessing to others every day. Amen.

2 CORINTHIANS 9:7

2 May

Father, You have given me seed to sow.
You are exponentially multiplying my seed.
Your blessings make me wealthy so that I can
always be generous in my giving. My generosity in
giving and serving others produce prayers
of thanksgiving for the generosity you
have shown me. Amen.

2 Corinthians 9:10-11

May 3

Father, I honor you with my daily blessings of service to others and my commitment in spreading the good news of Christ. I thank you for the prayers others pray on my behalf. You have placed compassion in my heart to serve others because of the kindness you have shown me. I am blessed to be a blessing. I thank you for this gift that mere words cannot describe. Amen.

Proverbs 11:25

Luke 6:38

4 May

Father, Regardless of whatever state
I may be in, I find reassurance in knowing
you are always with me. Thank you for your
unfailing love and presence. I unequivocally
know there is absolutely nothing that separates,
or will ever separate, you or your love from me.
Absolutely nothing! Amen.

Romans 8:35-39

May 5

Father, Your unfailing love is overwhelming. Whether I am abased or exalted, I know you are with me and providing for my every need. I am thankful for your unfailing loving-kindness and tender mercies that are new every morning. Great is your faithfulness. Amen.

LAMENTATIONS 3:22-23

6 May

Father, Your supernatural power is working in and through me. Men are clueless about the nature of who I am. They don't understand what is going on in my body, mind, spirit and soul. I don't place my confidence in man's report; I place it in yours. Your report breathes life in me because in you I live, move and function in the very essence of my being. I will live and not die so that I can proclaim your Word. Amen.

Acts 17:28

May 7

Father, I am so excited about today.
I woke up! I felt the breath of life in my body!
I knew I had another day to maximize your
awesome gift of life by using my intellectual
property in providing Kingdom solutions
to make this world a better place to live,
work, play and worship. Amen.

Psalm 3:5

8 May

Father, Today, I will act. Today,
I will make a difference. Today,
I will no longer settle for mediocrity.
Today, I will do all I need to do with
a spirit of excellence and integrity.
Today, I will celebrate the success
inherent in today. Amen.

PHILIPPIANS 4:4

May 9

Father, If you clothe the lilies and feed the ravens, how much more would you do for me? I will not be anxious about tomorrow because today I have enough to be concerned about. I will no longer allow procrastination to be the ruler of today. My courage and confidence in maximizing today, by doing it even in the midst of fear, makes me more than a conqueror over procrastination. It may be a thief, but procrastination no longer robs me of my time, skills or success of today. Amen.

MATTHEW 6:33-34

10 May

Father, Everything that was meant for my bad, you have already turned around for my good. All things are working together for my good. Even those things that are perceived to be bad are in alignment with your purpose for me. I am moving forward, living life to its fullest with confidence and courage. Regardless of what may happen, you are working it out for my good. That is what I know. That is what I believe. Amen.

ROMANS 8:28

May 11

Father, You make all things great
in your time. My greatness is in the fullness
of your time. The fullness of your time
makes me great in one area today and another
tomorrow. Every day, I will celebrate the
greatness in the fullness of your time
for that respective day. Amen.

ECCLESIASTES 3:11

12 May

Father, I'm excited about celebrating my mother. I'm excited that my mother loved me so much that she teamed up with you to make sure I'd become all you envisioned. I'm excited that my mother did not abort me, but endured the gestation period to welcome me into this world so that I could fulfill my potential. I'm excited that my mother nurtured me and taught me to believe in myself and, even more importantly, to believe and trust you. I'm excited about the blessed gift you have given me and others. Thank you for mothers as we celebrate mothers. Amen.

Luke 1:28

May 13

Father, I'm excited that you are doing more than everything I could ever imagine. It excites me to know that my dreams, regardless of how lofty they may be, are nothing in comparison to what you will really do. I dreamed and now I am acting on them. Thank you, God!
Amen.

EPHESIANS 3:20

14 May

Father, After experiencing such tremendous loss, I didn't think I would ever experience joy again. Time heals the heartache of loss. My sorrow turned into joy and my memories turned into priceless keepsakes. Thank you for turning my deepest pain into joyful dancing and covering me in such a brilliant light of joy and happiness. Amen.

PSALM 30:11-12

May 15

Father, This is a tremendous lost. We look to you for courage and strength to make it. We don't have all of the answers as to why, in your infinite wisdom, you chose to call our loved ones home. Yet, we nestle in the reassurance that your oil-of-joy is our strength and for the spirit of heaviness, you have given us a garment of praise. Amen.

ISAIAH 61:3

16 May

Father, We don't mourn like the world mourns. We have a reassurance that we will meet our loved ones again. Although they are absent from their bodies, they are forever in your presence. We may cry because we will miss laughing, talking, sharing and just being in their company. But, we rejoice in knowing they are no longer trapped in this earthly vessel. They are free to soar in your presence! Amen.

1 Thessalonians 4:13-18

May 17

Father, Though we have gone through the shadows of death, we are not afraid to keep moving forward. When that unwelcomed stranger called death pays a visit and snatches our loved ones away from us, we know that your Son, Jesus, conquered death. Oh death, where is your sting? Oh grave, where is your victory? Our joy comes in knowing that our loved ones live and dwell with you because your Son overcame it all. Amen.

PSALM 23

18 May

Father, The course may have been difficult at times, but we know our loved ones ran the race, finished the course and always kept the faith. Now they stand in front of you to receive their heavenly prize. We find solace in knowing that one day, we will see them again. We know that, through this process of healing, you are strengthening us day-by-day and moment by moment. Amen.

2 Timothy 4:7

May 19

Father, When it rains, it pours! I thank you for the overwhelming downpour of showers of blessing that overtake me. I look up to Heaven and exclaim with all my might, "Rain down on me! Blessings, rain down on me!" I am drenched! I am so excited! I am so happy! I am so blessed! I am so in love with you for showering me daily with blessings chocked-full of your promises. Thank you for prosperous wisdom and a wealth-filled life of possibilities!
Hallelujah! Amen!

EZEKIEL 34:26

20 MAY

Father, I woke up this morning, knowing that the celebration continues. We will sing! We will dance! We will shout, "Hallelujah!" It is a time of praise! It is a time of intense worship unto you as we celebrate the gift you gave us of the life and legacy of our loved one. Amen.

PSALM 126

May 21

Father, How much more joy can you
bestow upon us? Our way of escape through
this process is your illimitable oil of joy.
Oh, how we bask in knowing you have
bestowed us with an overabundance
of joy to propel us forward.
We just thank you. Amen.

ECCLESIASTES 7:1-2

22 May

Father, More than anything, I love you. I may not always understand, but I know you are a sovereign God who knows the beginning from the end. You know the day we are born, as well as everything you placed inside of us to succeed. You also know the day we will leave this earth. What we do in the between time is what matters most. Bless me to fulfill my purpose with passion, exemplified by the dash that links my birth date and my death date. Amen.

Psalm 139:12-14

Ecclesiastes 7:1-2

May 23

Father, Every day, I become stronger.
I've put on the garment of praise. It is time to
rejoice in you. It is time to celebrate life.
It is time to glorify you as I celebrate
the gift of life. Amen.

Isaiah 61:3

24 May

Father, Teach me how to manage my time effectively, as an entrepreneur who also works another job. Each day, bless me to have balance in my life as I juggle these two obligations with efficiency and excellence. Bless me to value and appreciate my job, as a catalyst in realizing my dream as an entrepreneur. Amen.

Psalm 90:12

May 25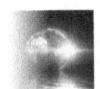

Father, We remember and celebrate the lives of the many women and men who gave their lives for this country and our freedom. Bless those families who have lost their loved ones as they remember their unselfish commitment to this country. We celebrate their bravery and courage in battle. Amen.

MATTHEW 5:4

26 May

Father, Our country celebrates its fallen heroes who gave their lives. Bless us to never forget the unselfish sacrifice of the lives of so many women and men who bravely defended this country, so we can safely enjoy life. Amen.

Hebrews 12:1-2

May 27

Father,

We remember the sacrifices of so many women and men who died while in battle. We also remember those who died from wounds inflicted during their service to this country. Their sacrifices enable us to experience freedom. Let us never forget that their sacrifices ensure that we are one nation under your watchful eye. Because of them, we experience life, liberty, justice and the pursuit of happiness. You, God Almighty, provide for our common defense and general welfare. You bestow blessings of liberty upon us today and forevermore. Amen.

GALATIANS 5:1 JOHN 8:32

28 May

Father, Thank you for the unity of my family. We need each other. I come against anything that tries to separate us. Bless us to band together and celebrate the differences that make us one. We will stand together in united love. Bless us to work together, play together and, most importantly, pray together. When we do, we stay together. Amen.

Psalm 133

May 29

Father, I am determined to succeed today. I am determined to maximize the 86,400 seconds of today with passion and fervor. Today, I will seize the moment! Today, I will use my time wisely! Today, I will maximize my efforts! Today, I will be diligent! Today, I will be relentless to succeed in everything I do! Amen.

PSALM 90:12

30 May

Father, Each day, I celebrate life. I celebrate it because once again, you blew the breath of life into me, enabling me to fulfill my purpose in the earth. I don't take my life for granted, but I maximize each moment as though it was my last. No longer will I procrastinate. I will do all that you have placed inside of me to do. I will do it with fervency and with passion. Amen.

Psalm 118:24

Psalm 15:15 Romans 12:11

May 31

Father, Dreams are for dreamers as much as dreamers are for dreams. I dream big. I take big actions to fulfill my dreams. I know that you are taking even bigger actions, ensuring that all my dreams come true in my lifetime. You placed these dreams inside of me. Thank you, God, for my dreams and the fulfillment of every one! Amen.

NUMBERS 12:6

PSALM 14:6 EPHESIANS 3:20

JUNE

Prayer opens your mind and liberates you to receive the abundance of God. You become more focused to hear God's instructions and to quickly do them as a marketplace influencer.

GALATIANS 5:1

June 1

Father, There is no lack in my life. Every financial need is met. You have given me the double defensive protection of money and wisdom while I am still living. Wisdom is the ultimate defense that enables me to manage my affairs with integrity. Wealth and riches are in my house. I dwell in the wealthy place of abundance and prosperity. Amen.

ECCLESIASTES 7:11-12

# 2 JUNE

Father, I am not a double-minded person.
A double-minded person is unstable in all of
his or her ways. I have a sound mind with
thoughts that propel me to accomplish great feats
on behalf of humankind. I have taken on your
mindset and, in doing so, I have tapped
into the wellspring of illimitable possibilities.
I am unstoppable. Amen.

JAMES 1:5

June 3

Father, You've anointed me for greatness.
Greatness is all I will achieve. Everything
I set my hands to do is already successful
because your favor and blessings of greatness
are on everything I do. Amen.

PSALM 90:17

4 June

Father, More than anything, I feel fire shut up in my bones, igniting me with passion to do the impossible. Obstacles and barriers no longer prevent me from achieving success. I am successful because you said I am successful. Whatever you say I am, that is who I am. You define me and my destiny. I walk boldly and confidently in your definition to achieve success. Amen.

PSALM 37:24

JOSHUA 1:9 JEREMIAH 20:9

June 5

Father, Those people who said I will not be successful were totally wrong. I nullify every negative word that has been spoken over my life. I know I will accomplish immeasurable feats because you are an exceeding God. You will do more than I can ever imagine. I live in the realm of impossibilities. Amen.

ISAIAH 54:17

EPHESIANS 3:20

6 June

Father, My mind has been cleared of negative thoughts. I am running with the vision you placed inside of me. I've paced myself for success. I know I will win because I will never, ever give up. I will achieve and become everything you have envisioned.
Amen.

1 Corinthians 9:24-27
Philippians 3:13-14

June 7

Father, The cobwebs of defeat have been flushed from my mind. For poverty, you have given me wealth. For sickness and disease, you have given me health. For low self-esteem, you have given me confidence. I will never cast away my confidence because the rewards are too great. I am successful in everything I do. Amen.

HEBREWS 10:35-36

8 June

Father, Every day, I wake up determined to persevere and never give up. There is nothing that can stop me from progressing full-speed ahead to achieve my goals. I am a formidable force to be reckoned with because I have teamed up with you. I have embraced all the greatness you envisioned for me. Amen.

1 Corinthians 15:58

June 9

Father, If I can conceive it in my mind, I know I will do more than achieve it. I have connected my thoughts with your infinite intelligent thoughts. I know I am more than equipped to accomplish the impossible. Amen.

MARK 11:23

PHILIPPIANS 4:13

10 June

Father, My words transform my mind. No longer will negative thoughts prevent me from achieving greatness. My positive conscious thoughts of prosperity and wealth propel me to success uncommon to the average mind. Amen.

Romans 12:2

June 11

Father, Today, I think I can. I believe I can. I can do it. I think I will. I believe I will. I will do it. I think I can finish. I believe I can finish. I am already finished. Amen.

PHILIPPIANS 3:14

12 June

Father, I thank you for waking me up this morning, in my right mind and in excellent health. This is the day you have made. I will rejoice and be glad in it. I am prospering and in health, even as my soul prospers. I am excited about the opportunities that today will bring. I will seize them and maximize them with passion and purpose. Amen.

Psalm 118:24

3 John 1:2

June 13

Father, Iron sharpens iron. You have blessed me with someone who is willing to sharpen me for the greatness you envisioned. Bless me to have an ear to hear and receive instruction because I need their coaxing and support. I know this person has been divinely placed in my life because of your infinite wisdom to make sure I proceed confidently and successfully into my destiny as I fulfill my purpose. Amen.

Proverbs 12:17

Proverbs 18:24   Hebrews 10:24-25a

14 June

Father, From the day I entered this world,
I have been on a journey that is not just
about me, but about everyone I encounter.
One day, I will no longer have breath in my body.
Oh, please bless me to have contributed positively
during my lifetime. Bless me to have touched
someone's life. After I've taken my last breath,
bless my life to continually make a difference.
Allow my life to be a beacon of light that directs
others to you. Every day, I endeavor
to make my life count in creating a better world
for all humankind. Amen.

ROMANS 12:10-12
ECCLESIASTES 5:18   ACTS 20:24

June 15

Father, We celebrate our fathers. Regardless if they were great fathers, average fathers or absent fathers, we celebrate that they connected with our mothers in creating us. For that, we thank our fathers and ask you to keep them under your watchful eye. We celebrate our fathers for the things that they taught us, knowingly and unknowingly. Simply stated, we celebrate our fathers because they are our fathers. Without them, we would not be here. In our celebration, we celebrate you, our Heavenly Father. Thank you for loving us and for creating us to achieve greatness. Amen.

1 CORINTHIANS 4:15

16 June

Father, Daily, you bless me with wisdom, understanding, counsel, might and knowledge in order to break away from limited thinking, inefficiency and ineffectiveness. I burst past these limitations as I become more efficient and effective in achieving my goals and transforming my mindset. I expect success each and every day in everything that I do. Amen.

Isaiah 11:2

Romans 12:2

June 17

Father, My habits dictate my success. I am establishing productive habits for optimum success. I will set goals in order for my habits to transform into a way of life. I will do them even when I don't feel like doing them. I overcome the habit of doing nothing and will do something every day in order to achieve success in every area of my life. Amen.

PSALM 90:12

PROVERBS 22:29

18 June

Father, Bless me to be an effective manager.
Teach me how to prioritize for success.
Moment-by-moment, day-by-day, I am
becoming stronger, wiser, more efficient, and
more effective and disciplined in all that I do.
I have learned to number my days so
I can apply my heart to wisdom. Amen.

PSALM 90:12

June 19

Father, Bless me with the ability to celebrate the maturation process of progress. Give me the ability to celebrate each step as I learn new things. Give me the patience to wait on you before moving forward to the next. Bless me not to become so anxious that I jump over steps, only for me to go back and complete them. Bless me not to get stuck in the process by remaining at a step too long. Help me to proceed with confidence as you guide me to success. Amen.

Joshua 1:9
Proverbs 3:6

20 June

Father, Bless me with the ability to listen.
Bless me with stillness inside of me to listen
with compassion rather than listening to speak.
Bless me as I communicate with others.
Help us to talk with each other,
not at each other. Amen.

PSALM 46:10

June 21

Father, I am not consumed with perfection because perfection is only in you. I do live a life rooted in a spirit of excellence. It is this spirit of excellence that propels me to do the right thing, even when I don't want to do it. It is this spirit of excellence where perfection no longer paralyzes and immobilizes my success. Amen.

DANIEL 6:1

22 June

Father, You are transforming me from the inside out. Old paradigms are fading away and new ones are emerging. These new paradigms are shaping my character for success in every area of my life. I no longer view things from a negative paradigm, but from a positive one. This enables me to overcome every obstacle that may be set before me. Amen.

ROMANS 12:2

June 23

Father, Bless me to embrace the opinions of others. It may not be what I envisioned or what I think, but bless me to understand their opinions as you bless them to understand mine.
In the process, we will be able to respect the differences that make us one in coming to a consensus for success. Amen.

PROVERBS 15:22
PROVERBS 19:20 PROVERBS 12:15

24 June

Father, Family is so important. We need each other. Bless us to band together and be able to celebrate our sameness and the differences that make us one. There will be no strife, confusion or division. We will stand together in oneness of voice, oneness of vision, oneness of purpose and oneness of mission as we achieve both individual and collective victories. We are a formidable force to be reckoned with because you are in our midst. Amen.

PSALM 133

June 25

Father, I am working on this project and I need your help. Please give me the direction I need for it to be successful. Reveal to me anything that will prohibit me from being successful. Bless me to work effectively with others to ensure we are a successful team and that we meet all deadlines. Thank you for your guidance and direction. Amen.

PROVERBS 16:3, 9

PROVERBS 3:5-6

26 JUNE

Father, Life is about living! I am going to live my life to the fullest! Each day, I will wake up with a plan of action to succeed. Each day, I will do something to take care of my body so I can be in peak shape to perform and live a healthy life. I will respect health as much as I respect healing. I will eat right. I will work out daily. I will dwell only on positive things that bring life. Each day, I will live life to its fullest! Amen.

PHILIPPIANS 4:8

June 27

Father, We experience great sorrows in life.
But as each day passes, we become stronger.
I am amazed at the resiliency you placed inside
of us to overcome the greatest of losses. I thank
you for your infinite wisdom you've placed inside
of me. Thank you for the ability to mourn and
to stay on track to achieve all the great things you
envisioned for me. Amen.

LAMENTATIONS 3:22-23

28 June

Father, I am so excited about my life. Apparently, so are you. Your excitement about the great contributions I will make in the earth started before I was born. You have placed inside of me everything I need to succeed. I will take what you have placed inside of me and multiply it so I can I accomplish all the great things you envisioned. Amen.

JEREMIAH 1:5 2 KINGS 4:2

JUNE 29

Father, Life is interesting. I wake up each morning with a spirit of expectation. I wake up because of you—the Life Giver. It is my desire not to squander this gift that you have given me. Regardless of the trials and tribulations of life, I will maximize my days as I use them wisely. I will team up with you to create a better world to live, work, play and worship. Amen.

PSALM 90:12 JOB 12:4
PSALM 37:34 HEBREWS 11:1

30 June

Father, Everything I need is inside of me,
waiting to burst forth. It began with
a dream-seed. Now it is blooming where
I planted that dream-seed. It is blossoming
into a bouquet of unparalleled
accomplishments and success. Amen.

ISAIAH 55:10
JOB 33:15-16 GENESIS 37:6

JULY

Prayer enables you to move circumspectly in pursuit of your passion. All the while, you unequivocally know that giving up is never an option. Prayer liberates you and sets you free from issues that have held you hostage and have kept you from experiencing spiritual abundance, wholeness and wealth.

1 Chronicles 28:20

Galatians 6:9

1 July

Father, Apply your spiritual saliva on my eyes so I can see clearly. No longer will the blurriness of vision prevent me from moving forward. Now, I am able to proceed confidently in the path you paved for me. With each step, I possess all that you envisioned as you make my way prosperous and I experience good success in all I do. Amen.

MARK 8:22-25

JOSHUA 1:9

July 2

Father, Bless us to work together and effectively communicate with each other so we can accomplish phenomenal feats we could never do alone. In your infinite wisdom, you didn't just create us to function alone; you created us to use our intellectual properties to achieve greatness. With every victory, we celebrate the synergistic win because when one person wins, we all win! Thank you, God, for making every one of us winners! Amen.

GENESIS 2:18

EXODUS 18:34

3 July

Father, I embrace the fullness of life with vibrancy of positive energy. It begins as a wellspring of positive energy that flows out to others. It emancipates me to generously help, give and celebrate others in pursuit of my desires and dreams. I endeavor to make the world a better place to live, work, play and worship. Amen.

Luke 6:38

July 4

Father, Today we celebrate our country's independence as a free country. Bless us to turn back to the foundation on which this country was founded, which is your Word. Bless us to never forget that it was the passion of its forefathers and their commitment to your Word that allow us to enjoy freedom like no other country. Bless us never to forget that it is the Godly-heritage of this country that has made it great. Bless each of us to walk out our freedom to the right of religion and worship. Keep this country covered under your blood of protection. Amen.

GALATIANS 5:1

2 CHRONICLES 7:14

5 July

Father, My ability to gaze into the mirror and envision myself as you do, enables me to realize that I am not an island. You have blessed me with bountiful, success-inspired relationships. Every day, I celebrate the differences that make us one. In this oneness of celebration, we are able to achieve unparalleled success—not just individually, but collectively. Amen.

1 CORINTHIANS 12

July 6

Father, When I gaze into the mirror, I see the person you see. I'm able to peer beyond this dirt suit of a body to envision the awesome person you have blessed with immeasurable gifts and talents to soar to greatness. No longer do I allow the gravitational limitations of this world to prevent me from soaring to heights unimaginable to the common mind. Amen.

PSALM 139:13-16

ISAIAH 40:31

7 July

Father, My relationships with others don't complete me, they complement me. My relationship with you completes and complements me. My foundational dominion of self-discipline is built on the interdependence of my relationships with you and others. It enables me to not only respect and love me, but to respect and love you with all my heart, mind and soul, and to love and respect others as well. Amen.

1 Peter 4:8-10
1 John 4:7-11

July 8

Father, I thank you for the gift of the present.
It is such an awesome present, as it ushers me into
your presence. In the awesomeness of
your presence, I embrace intimacy that flows
seamlessly into unbridled passion. I nurture and
cherish the gift of the present, which enables
me to bask in your presence. Amen.

EXODUS 20:8

JEREMIAH 17:21-22 PSALM 46:10

9 July

Father, While I was in the valley of the shadow of death, it seemed like it was unbearable. I thought I would not make it through. Because of it, I am able to bask in the knowledge of where I've been. I'm able to embrace and celebrate the gift of the present with a clearer view as to where I'm going. For this, I'm thankful for the valley moments that prepared me for the mountaintop victories. Amen.

PSALM 23

July 10

Father, Expectation is making me wait! I know I am primed for promotion and elevation. Thank you for the favor you have given me with others. I know you have already prepared me for this promotion. Everything I need to succeed is already inside of me. This expectation of elevation excites me! I just can't hide it! I simply love you for trusting me with such an awesome responsibility. Amen.

Psalm 27:14
Psalm 75:6-7

11 July

Father, Great things are happening!
I'm so excited! I passionately embrace all
of the great things happening in my life.
My horizon of success extends beyond the
limitations of my mind. I am more and more
confident in my capabilities to succeed each
and every day. Amen.

PHILIPPIANS 1:7
JEREMIAH 29:11

July 12

Father, Every day, my mind is being transformed. I am not the same person I was a year ago. I have no intentions on being the same person I am today, a year from now.

Each day, I embrace thoughts that propel me to embrace all the great things you envisioned for me. Every day when I gaze into the mirror, I see what you saw. I'm glad to be alive! Amen.

ROMANS 12:1-2

13 July

Father, I am no longer oppressed by those
who think they have the authority to close me out
from the great things you have for my life.
I have dreamed and can envision all you created
me to be. I am breaking out of the windows,
trying to separate me from the abundant life you
envisioned. The violent takes it by force. No longer
will I sit idly by and allow others to shut me out.
I am a window breaker! I am taking it by force!
Amen.

2 Kings 7:2
Jeremiah 9:21 Matthew 11:12

July 14

Father, I have lacked wisdom long enough about the wall of separation of church and state. I know that you have a mandate for me to go into the entire world, which also includes the marketplace. Bless me to represent you well as a marketplace influencer for the Kingdom of God to those who may not otherwise have an encounter with you. Amen.

MATTHEW 28:19-20 EPHESIANS 4:1
EPHESIANS 6:5-9 TITUS 3:1

15 July

Father, I have made a decision that the "big bang" of my life starts right now. I am turning away from every negative habit that prevents me from enjoying the "big bang" of my existence. My sudden success is chocked with every positive habit I do every single day. Negative habits no longer have dominion over me. I overcome them daily with habits that foster a blueprint for unparalleled success. My sudden success may be a shock to others. However, I know my "big bang" started when I planted habitual positive seeds so I can reap an abundant harvest of success. Amen.

Proverbs 10:4 Isaiah 48:3
1 Corinthians 10:23 Philippians 3:13-14

July 16

Father, My unwavering trust is in you. I will not place my confidence in the temporary things of this world because they fail me every time. However, I place my endless trust in you because you always have my best interest in mind and in your heart. I am the apple of your eye. I place more trust in you than in myself. Amen.

ROMANS 12:2

PSALM 17:8

17 July

Father, Life is all about living it with unbridled passion! I am living life in total abandonment as I pursue my dreams and desires with passion and fervency. I will not look back, but I press toward the high mark you have for my life. I will no longer aim low. I will aim high beyond the sky because there are footprints on the moon. Amen.

1 CORINTHIANS 9:24-27
PHILIPPIANS 3:13-14

July 18

Father, Your positive, life-giving energy supersedes any negative, depleting energy of this world. Greater is He who is inside of me than what is in this world. Your Spirit dwells inside of me, energizing me to become all you envisioned.

I know it is great because what you have envisioned for me is a bright future, paved with one successful victory after another. Amen.

JEREMIAH 29:11
1 JOHN 4:4

19 July

Father, My will to succeed is overwhelming! know I can do all things through Christ who strengthens me. It is this strength that causes me to have your joy, which will not allow me to give up. I know my victory is imminent. I refuse to relinquish my will to succeed to fear. I am fearless and I am victorious! Amen.

2 Timothy 1:7
Philippians 4:13

July 20

Father, I live in a temporary world, but I operate with an eternal mindset. I will not allow the temporariness of this world to prevent me from being eternally optimistic in fulfilling my desired mission. The mandate of the mission supersedes the finiteness of time. I am able to accomplish feats that are unimaginable to the human mind. Amen.

ROMANS 12:2
EPHESIANS 3:20

21 July

Father, Thank you for giving me fervency of spirit that empowers me with strength and potency to accomplish my goals, make necessary decisions, and act on them. My passion drives me beyond the fear of impotency into a place of potency in fulfilling my potential. Amen.

ECCLESIASTES 11:6A
ROMANS 12:11   PROVERBS 10:4

July 22

Father, Sometimes the vicissitudes of life appear to be overpowering. But I gain strength in knowing I will make it no matter what. You have strengthened me to endure. My persistence in the midst of it all enables me to overcome insurmountable odds. I thank you for never leaving my side, as I progressively move toward my goals in fulfillment of my purpose. Amen.

ROMANS 8:28

REVELATION 12:11

23 July

Father, I walk in healthy fear as I offer reverence to you in all things. This fear is where the wellspring of wisdom gushes forth in abundance. The more I reverence you, the more I am blessed with an abundance of wisdom to get wealth. I will be successful in whatever I set my hands to do. Amen.

DEUTERONOMY 18:8
ISAIAH 11:2 PSALM 1:3

July 24

Father, My reverence of you is a wellspring of life. Every day, I make a conscious decision to walk in your commandments—line upon line and precept upon precept. It is your commandments that guide me to unparalleled success in every area of my life. Amen.

ISAIAH 28:10

25 July

Father, In the instability of our world, I find my security in you. You are my refuge and my strength. I find solace in knowing that regardless of what is going on, you are always with me—providing me with peace, stability and security in an unstable, volatile world. Amen.

PSALM 118:8-9

PSALM 20:7 PHILIPPIANS 4:19

July 26

Father, There is absolutely nothing in this world that will cause me to be distracted from my mission. You have placed the mission inside of me, and I will protect it by staying focused and committed to accomplishing it, until I take my last breath. Amen.

ECCLESIASTES 5:18

GALATIANS 1:15

27 July

Father, How can I proceed without a clear mission of purpose? I pray that you would enlighten me of who you created me to be. I embrace my mission and pursue it with passion. I will write it so I can see it every day as it impassions me to boldly and purposefully progress toward it and in it. Amen.

JEREMIAH 29:11
HABAKKUK 2:1

July 28

Father, No longer will my indecision prevent me from fulfilling my desires. I will not allow fear to stop me from making the necessary decisions, as I progress toward my goals. I will not be double-minded and unstable in my decisions. I will do it with decisiveness, courage and confidence. Amen.

JAMES 1:8
HEBREWS 10:35-36 ECCLESIASTES 11:4

29 July

Father, I refuse to be entangled again with bad habits and things that prevent me from experiencing the fullness of your freedom. Each day, I embrace my unalienable rights to an abundant life, liberty and the pursuit of happiness. Daily, I apply your Word, which propels me into absolute freedom that exceeds the limitations of this world. Amen.

GALATIANS 5:1
2 CORINTHIANS 3:17
ROMANS 6:14
1 PETER 2:16

July 30

Father, The windows of Heaven are flung
open and you are pouring out a financial blessing
that is overtaking me. I bring all my tithes and
offerings to take care of your house. Therefore, I
know you are doing exceedingly, abundantly more
in taking care of my house. Your showers
of blessing keep raining down on me
day after day. Amen.

MALACHI 3:10-11

EZEKIEL 34:26

31 July

Father, Money cometh to me from everywhere right now. It is answering all of my financial needs. There is no lack in my life because I dwell in the realm of the overflow. A thunderous outpouring of money overtakes me. Shower me with your financial blessing. Lack no longer makes me ashamed because of the abundance of your showers of blessing. Amen.

PHILIPPIANS 4:19
EZEKIEL 34:26

AUGUST

Prayer enables you to be
transformed from the inside out,
into a new creation where God can
always bring out the best in you.
The limitations of this world
no longer prevent you from
accomplishing success as
a marketplace influencer.

ROMANS 12:1-2

1 August

Father, My desire is to become the creation you envisioned me to become. It is in this restorative process that I am made into a new creation, from the inside out. It is only when I'm willing to totally empty myself for a renewed spirit and mind that I am able to experience the fullness of you. Amen.

2 Corinthians 5:17

August 2

Father, I have a project that overwhelms me. Bless me to tackle this project with courage and confidence. Reveal to me how to map it out in incremental steps that take the overwhelming feelings away. Provide me with the necessary resources and people I need to successfully complete it on time and within budget. I will hold fast to my profession of faith and will not cast away my confidence because it has great rewards. My complete confidence is in you, which in turn enables me to have confidence in my capabilities. Amen.

1 Chronicles 28:20
Hebrews 10:35-36

3 August

Father, Bless me to be able to deal with difficult people. Reveal to me who they are in your eyes in order for me to be able to effectively work with them. Whenever we need to confer with each other, intervene so we can talk to each other and not at each other. Bless us to be able to hear each other and to respectfully respond to each other. Amen.

1 Samuel 24:12-13

Colossians 4:6   Ephesians 4:6

Proverbs 15:1   Proverbs 17:14

Philippians 2:1-4

AUGUST 4

Father, I did not sleep well last night, but I still have to complete these assignments. Please keep me awake, aware and alert so I will not make any mistakes. Provide me with your supernatural energy and wherewithal to get through this day. Bless me to be attentive in the meetings I attend throughout the day, in order for me to provide valuable input and to walk away with increased knowledge. Amen.

ISAIAH 40:27-31

PSALM 138:3 PHILIPPIANS 2:13

5 August

Father, I have to devise strategies for success. I don't know where to start or how to begin. People are depending on me. Provide me with your divine wisdom, understanding, counsel, strength and knowledge of what needs to be included. Bless me to overcome the fear of starting the project. You are with me every step of the way, and you will be with me until the day of completion. Knowing that you will never leave or forsake me propels me forward to achieve illimitable success. Amen.

Philippians 1:7

Isaiah 11:2

August 6

Father, My eating habits are preventing me from being as successful as I need to be. I feel sluggish and lethargic. Teach me how to establish healthy eating habits so I can perform at my optimum potential. I know you have provided me with food, but that doesn't mean I should be under its control. No longer will I make unhealthy food choices because my body has been bought with a price. I conquer unhealthy cravings as I prosper in health, even as my soul prospers.
Amen.

1 Corinthians 6:12-13
3 John 1:2

7 AUGUST

Father, Thank you for teaching me to count it all joy, when I enter into diverse temptations. Patience is having its most perfect work in me. As I learn to be more patient with myself, I also exhibit that same patience with others. Teach me how to wait on you, knowing that even if it appears as though the promise may be delayed, it is not a denial. It will manifest in the fullness of your time. Give me the strength to endure, be productive and prosper in the meantime. Amen.

JAMES 1:1-4

PSALM 27:14 HABAKKUK 2:3

August 8

Father, Give me a spirit of perseverance and persistence as I run this race so I can hear, "Well done." Don't let me give up when things get hard. Keep me focused on the goal that lies ahead. You said to forget those things that are behind and press toward the mark of your high calling. Bless me not to allow circumstances, situations, experiences and people to keep me from completing the corresponding actions that lead to the success you envisioned for me every day. Amen.

MATTHEW 25:21
PHILIPPIANS 3:13-14

9 August

Father, I know iron sharpens iron. There are so many things I have been trying to accomplish, but to no avail. I do need someone to help propel me to experience all you created me to be, and for me to do the same for them. Bless me with an open heart to receive, not only words of encouragement, but words of rebuke on my pathway to unparalleled success. Amen.

Proverbs 27:17
Hebrews 10:24-25a
Proverbs 27:9

August 10

Father, The hurt from sticks and stones pales in comparison to the negative words said to me or about me. These negative words weren't supposed to hurt me, yet they scarred me for life. Had it not been for your Word and the redeeming blood of Jesus, I would still be scarred and lost in a world of despair and hopelessness. I thank you for, daily, revealing your words of life to me. It is these words that catapult me into a realm of expectation and an abundant life that I never imagined I could ever experience. I love you for loving me. Amen.

JAMES 3:5 PROVERBS 18:21 JOB 6:25
EPHESIANS 6:17B ISAIAH 55:11
LUKE 4:4 HEBREWS 4:12

11 August

Father, I need you to cut away all of those
dead issues that are preventing me from being
all you created me to be. Daily teach me how
to apply your Word to these circumstances.
They will no longer cause me pain and anguish.
I am dependent on you. Each day, I seek you
for instruction and guidance, as your Word propels
me to walk in the success I once only dreamed
about. I thank you that I am walking into
what you envisioned for me from the
beginning of time. Amen.

Isaiah 18:5

John 15:1-3

August 12

Father, You are love. Bless me to walk in the greatest two commandments—to love you with all my heart, mind and soul; and love my neighbor as I love myself. I know there is no condemnation for those who love the Lord and are called according to His purpose. Bless me not to be so critical that it affects my ability to love others and myself. In doing so, I will be able to see them as you see them. Teach me how to love as Jesus loved, to love my foes as I love my friends. Every place I go, I will celebrate others by showering them with love.
Amen.

MATTHEW 22:36-40

1 PETER 4:7-8   1 JOHN 4:18-21

13 August

Father, I behold you in all of your majestic glory and the awesomeness of your name, I Am that I Am. It is in the power of your spirit that I am able to do and become all you envisioned for me. It is in the power of your spirit that I am able to reach beyond myself to help others become all they can be. Amen.

Exodus 3:14-15
Psalm 5:11-12 Psalm 91:14-16
Isaiah 44:2a Romans 12:2
Psalm 138:8

August 14

Father, Thank you for your Sabbath presence. The gift of your presence is the best present because it ushers me into your presence. Bless me to make time just to be with you. Teach me how to be still and embrace all the beauty you have created in this world. Bless me to enjoy dwelling in your presence in order for me to be still so I can clearly hear your voice and your instruction, which propels me down the pathway of success. Amen.

MATTHEW 11:28-29

EXODUS 20:8 JEREMIAH 17:21-22

ISAIAH 58:13 MARK 2:27

PSALM 46:10

15 AUGUST

Father, I realize you are doing a new thing in my life and I'm ready to embrace it. No longer will I be afraid to walk away and walk into a new season. With your guidance, I know I will experience unimaginable success. It is because of this, I am releasing the familiar for the unfamiliar and I dare to begin again. Amen.

ISAIAH 43:18-19

ECCLESIASTES 3:1, 11

PSALM 1:3

August 16

Father, Thank you for transforming my mindset from an idle state of complacency to a spirit of expectancy, empowered by action. I know I am becoming all you have envisioned and I walk in the abundance of your promises and blessings. With this new mindset of expectancy, coupled with action, every gift and talent will be wisely used to glorify you daily as I experience success in every endeavor. Amen.

Job 12:4 Job 14:14b
Psalm 37:34 Psalm 31:24
Isaiah 54:17b
Acts 26:6 Hebrews 11:1

17 August

Father, Bless me to realize that I cannot accomplish anything by my might or will, but it is all by your spirit. It is in the stillness of the moment, where you are working everything out for my good. Just because something hasn't happened doesn't mean it will not happen. I will surrender, be still and know you have everything under control as you propel me down a path of incomprehensible success. Amen.

PSALM 46:10
ISAIAH 65:24 JAMES 4:13
ZECHARIAH 4:6B
MARK 3:39

August 18

Father, Bless me to realize that I cannot accomplish anything by my own might or power. It is all by your spirit. Teach me how to be still and know you are God. My being still enables you to work things out for my good and in your timing. Just because something hasn't happened as quickly as I want it to, doesn't mean you are denying me. I am confident in knowing that it is only a delay, not a denial. I will confidently and courageously be still. I know you have everything under control and everything is coming together for my good. Amen.

Psalm 46:10

Zechariah 4:6b Romans 8:28

19 August

Father, I celebrate the divine connections you have placed in my life. Every friendship has been instrumental for me to achieve and become all you envisioned. Bless me not to take these relationships for granted, but to nurture and cultivate them as each of us fulfills our destiny and purpose. Continue to bless us each day to provide strength, support and encouragement as we journey through the vicissitudes of life—regardless if the relationship is for a day, a month, a season or a lifetime. Amen.

PROVERBS 27:17

LUKE 1:42-43 PROVERBS 18:24

August 20

Father, Teach me to respect the talents and gifts of others and to celebrate the differences that make us one. Not so much to make them like me, but for us to work together to fulfill all you have placed inside each of us. Together, we become a formidable force to be reckoned with. Separately, we are more vulnerable and can't successfully accomplish nearly as much as we can together. A three-fold cord is not easily broken. Amen.

ECCLESIASTES 4:9-10
ECCLESIASTES 4:12   PROVERBS 27:17
PSALM 133:1   EXODUS 36:1

21 August

Father, Bless me to be a person who doesn't merely meditate on pure and good things, but to be a person of action. I don't just give lip service. I am a doer. In doing so, I know I will experience all you have for me as you make my way prosperous and I experience stupendous success. Amen.

JOSHUA 1:8
PHILIPPIANS 4:8 PSALM 1:2-3
ROMANS 12:2

August 22

Father, With every book I write, I commit my works to you. Bless my words to be like the pen of a skillful writer, as you anoint my hands to write every word you have spoken to me for publishing and widespread distribution. Everyone reading them, not just in this generation, but generations yet to be born, will be transformed to live out their destiny and fulfill their purpose. Amen.

Psalm 45:1
Psalm 68:11   Isaiah 30:8
Jeremiah 30:2

23 AUGUST

Father, Sometimes it appears as though there is so much to do and not enough time. Please help me to bring order into my life according to your will, not my own, so I can prioritize a myriad of tasks, projects and appointments, as well as family, and personal and business obligations. Please teach me to number my days so I can effectively manage the time you have allotted me wisely. Amen.

PSALM 90:12

EPHESIANS 5:15-17 PROVERBS 24:3-4

PROVERBS 24:27 LUKE 14:28-30

AUGUST 24

Father, Everything seems to be spiraling like a tornado, but I thank you for keeping me in perfect peace. I dwell in the midst of it all, but it doesn't dwell in me. Continue to bless me with peace that surpasses understanding as I continue to be victorious, even if I am in the eye of the storm. The center is where perfect peace abounds, as I stay focused on you. Amen.

PHILIPPIANS 4:7

ISAIAH 26:3   COLOSSIANS 3:15-16

25 August

Father, Sometimes I find myself idling away time when I know there are a myriad of tasks I need to accomplish. I beseech you to ignite passion in me to do what needs to be done. I decree and declare that procrastination, complacency, fear and lack-of-focus will no longer stop me from purposeful productivity in every aspect of my life. Amen.

Romans 8:37

Psalm 90:12

AUGUST 26

Father, Bless me in my determination to win. I am running this race to win, but sometimes, I need added strength to stay disciplined to do it every day. I know in order for me to be at my optimum game, I have to eat healthy and exercise. I thank you for diligence, determination, commitment and persistence to do it—even when I don't want to do it. Amen.

GALATIANS 5:22

1 CORINTHIANS 9:22-24   HEBREWS 12:1-2

27 August

Father, Every day, help me create a win-win environment by using my position, power, possessions, influence and character to establish a liberating environment where creativity flows. As a team, we will experience increased wisdom, knowledge, productivity and creativity in conceiving, believing and achieving the impossible. Amen.

2 Corinthians 3:17

Isaiah 11:2

August 28

Father, Bless me to turn my finger inwardly as opposed to always blaming others. Teach me how to lead by example. Rather than always looking for a scapegoat, teach me to first look inwardly—for not just the problems—but for the solutions as well. In turn, I will be able to provide compassionate and proactive leadership that creates unified solutions. Amen.

MATTHEW 7:3-5

29 AUGUST

Father, I have to give some of my team members some distressing news. Please place your hand on my mouth and put your words of compassion in my mouth, words that will transform a distressful situation into one of empowerment, enabling them to view it as an open door of opportunity for optimum success. Amen.

JEREMIAH 1:9
EPHESIANS 6:18-19

August 30

Father, I don't always know what to do in a situation where I manage your people. I do know that you will provide me with the wisdom, understanding, counsel, might and knowledge I need to make informed decisions that unify and build up the team to succeed. Amen.

Isaiah 11:2

Psalm 133:1

31 August

Father, You created me to be a leader of
strength, courage, decisiveness and humility.
I am anointed to lead others and encourage
them to perform at their highest potential.
I thank you for enabling me to celebrate those
you have placed under my authority in guiding
them to experience the greatness
you envisioned for them. Amen.

Ephesians 4:12
1 Peter 5:6   Matthew 23:11-12

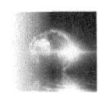

SEPTEMBER

Prayer ignites your faith, enabling
you to accomplish impossible feats, like
walking on water. You unequivocally know
you will not sink because you are defying
the gravitational pull of fear with the
supernatural power of great faith.

MATTHEW 14:29

1 SEPTEMBER

Father, There are no words that can express what it means to me that your Son, Jesus, gave His life that I can be free. It is this freedom that enables me to rise above the dictations of this world, allowing me to walk in absolute freedom and truth. More and more, I realize that His suffering, death and resurrection are the reason I have a right to an abundant and prosperous life. I look forward to living with you forever. Amen.

JOHN 8:36
JOHN 10:10

SEPTEMBER 2

Father, Teach me how to love as Jesus loved! My deepest desire is to love you with all my heart, mind and soul, and to love others as I love myself. I will display this love—not by mere words—but through action and deed. Through the love that flows from you to the Son, please pour that same love into me through your Holy Spirit. Then, I can be a reservoir, spreading agape love throughout the earth. Amen.

MARK 11:9

1 CORINTHIANS 13:1-3

SONG OF SOLOMON 8:6-7

1 JOHN 3:18-19

3 SEPTEMBER

Father, There are times when I have a hard time stepping out and just doing it. I seek great faith! Regardless of what may be happening, I will heed your instruction and honor your request. The only thing that prevents me from exercising radical faith is strongholds of fear. I know there is nothing too hard for you. I move confidently in overcoming every obstacle as I team up with you and am guided by the Holy Spirit. Whatever you instruct me to do, I will do it, even in the midst of the fear. Amen.

JEREMIAH 32:17
JEREMIAH 32:27

September 4

Father, I know you have provided me with a certain measure of faith, which increases with each trial and tribulation. I need your help as I proceed through life's ups and downs. I do not want you to view me as a person who lacks great faith. Teach me how to get out of the boat of fear and walk on the waters with exceeding faith to achieve the impossible. I can't begin to experience all you have for me until I walk by faith and not by blinding sight. Amen.

MATTHEW 14:29

HEBREWS 11:1 ROMANS 5:3-5

5 September

Father, I realize the vicissitudes of life are going to happen. Bless me to have a hunger and thirst for your Word. Help me to withstand every attack waged against me. Each day, my knowledge in your Word propels me to conquer any negative accusations and untruths that have been hurled at me. Teach me to apply your laws and commandments to every situation as I experience unparalleled success in all that you have purposed for me. Amen.

ROMANS 12:1-2
EPHESIANS 6:10-18
PROVERBS 8:35
ROMANS 8:28

SEPTEMBER 6

Father, I'm in search of my authentic self and only you can reveal to me who I am. Although I have searched in all the wrong places, I ask your forgiveness as I uncover those things which I thought were lost. I realize that you, in your infinite wisdom and sovereignty, placed everything I need inside of me. Now I have wisdom, understanding, counsel, might and knowledge about my desires, dreams and passions as I experience unbridled success. Amen.

MATTHEW 16:25
LUKE 15:8-10
JEREMIAH 29:11-14A
PROVERBS 8:35

7 SEPTEMBER

Father, I am tired of being angry. I don't know where the anger started. I know this anger must be plucked out from the root for me to move forward. I have been afraid to deal with these anger issues. I cry out for your mercy and grace to help me. It is your help that enables me to overcome negative emotions that drive me to repeatedly act out in anger. Although I realize how detrimental the anger has become, I find myself not being able to overcome it. I need you. Help me to relinquish the anger, so I can become all you envisioned. Amen.

ROMANS 7:14-25 PSALM 4:4
EPHESIANS 4:26-27 MATTHEW 5:22A

September 8

Father, I have placed so many things and people before you. I find myself continually searching and not finding the love that I desperately seek. As I move beyond the temporal love of this world, I embrace your eternal love. It is in this embrace that I feel the tenderness of your breath on my face, which exemplifies the intimate love I have yearned for all my life. It is unbelievable that it has always been there, just waiting for me to embrace it. Now I share a love affair that is totally beyond compare as I daily seek your embrace.

I love you. Amen.

JEREMIAH 29:13-14A JEREMIAH 29:13-14B
PSALM 27:8 PROVERBS 8:35 ROMANS 8:38-39
MARK 1:37 PROVERBS 8:17

9 SEPTEMBER

Father, I am responsible for everything I say. Give me the ability to refrain from idle conversations that can cause life-long debilitating effects for others as well as for myself. I will proclaim words of life, not death, especially the words I speak over and about children. My goal is to be a touchstone in others' lives so they can also be a touchstone in someone else's life. Allow my words to illuminate the light of Christ. Every word I speak will be in alignment with the life I profess to walk in Christ Jesus. Amen.

MATTHEW 12:36-37 1 CORINTHIANS 15:33
2 TIMOTHY 2:16 JOB 6:24 JOB 19:2 PSALM 19:14
PROVERBS 16:24 1 PETER 3:10 JAMES 3:5

SEPTEMBER 10

Father, The cares of this world sometimes overwhelm me. I find myself getting off course from what you would have for me to do. There are times when I place more importance on the concerns of men and their instruction than I do yours. Please help me to place my confidence in only you. You are the only one who has my destiny in your hands. More than anyone else, your plans are for me to have an expected end for a bright future with great success. Amen.

GALATIANS 5:10
PSALM 118:8-9 PROVERBS 25:19
1 KINGS 13:26 2 CHRONICLES 16:8-9

11 SEPTEMBER

Father, The imperfections in my life make me feel inadequate. Yet, I'm coming to realize these imperfections perfect me. If you took away all of my imperfections, there would be no hurdles. If there were no hurdles, I would not be able to leap over them as I glorify you. Others may not overcome because I wouldn't have my testimony of your perfecting grace. Bless me to celebrate my imperfections on my way to tremendous success. Amen.

2 CORINTHIANS 12:9

2 CORINTHIANS 3:5 2 CORINTHIANS 9:8

September 12

Father, Thank you for radical faith that overcomes the impossible. I know with you, all things are possible. It has nothing to do with common sense. Through conquering the senseless things, I am propelled into the realm of impossibility. Regardless of how lofty the impossible concept may be, I know I am well able to conquer it through you, who love me. Amen.

EPHESIANS 3:20
MATTHEW 17:20 MARK 10:27

13 SEPTEMBER

Father, Although you have provided unlimited resources for my success, there are times when I am just too afraid to use them. These fear-based tendencies prevent me from moving forward. You always had a clearly defined path for me. Teach me how to seek your guidance, and allow the Holy Spirit to lead and guide me. I will never forget that in your infinite wisdom, you masterfully placed your God-powered system inside of me, which leads and guides me down the path to unlimited possibilities and unparalleled success.

I love you, Holy Spirit! Amen.

JOHN 16:13 PROVERBS 3:6
JOHN 14:26 PSALM 139:3 PROVERBS 4:18
JOB 23:10 PSALM 18:30

September 14

Father, Every day, I seek your guidance. Without it, I seem to wander aimlessly, without direction. You, alone, know the path I need to be successful. You, alone, know the path that you envisioned for my life, even before the foundation of the earth.

When I walk the path you have for me, I am victorious in all I do. Please forgive me if I wander off the path, and gently guide me back onto the right one. Continue to lead and guide me down the path to the abundant life you envisioned before I was born. Amen.

Proverbs 3:6 Psalm 139:3
Proverbs 4:18 Job 23:10 Psalm 18:30
Psalm 25:10
Psalm 23:3-4 Joshua 1:8

15 September

Father, I am tired of betraying thoughts that prohibit me from serving you with all my heart, mind and soul. It is because of these diminutive self-defeating thoughts that I have been paralyzed. No more will my life be invaded and controlled by these negative thoughts. I will consume positive seeds from your Word. Daily, I will water them with prayer and meditation so as to transform these betraying thoughts of defeat to enormous thoughts of victory, propelling me into action and unparalleled success. Amen.

MATTHEW 6:19-21
MATTHEW 13:18-23 PSALM 139:17-18
JEREMIAH 29:11 MARK 7:18-21

September 16

Father, I have written the vision. Now it's time to implement it. No longer will I allow fear to harness me from unleashing and fulfilling my potential and doing what I need to do. You equipped me for greatness and I am well able to accomplish anything set before me. I will no longer get stuck in preparation, but I will set my sight on a victorious finish. I am persuaded that everything I need, you have already provided for my unsurpassed success. Amen.

1 Chronicles 28:20 Habakkuk 2:2-3
Revelation 3:8 1 Corinthians 9:24
1 Corinthians 9:25-26 Ecclesiastes 3:11-12
Philippians 3:12-14

17 SEPTEMBER

Father, There are so many things that are contrary to your Word. The negative messages are pervasive. Keep my thoughts, mind and heart stayed on you. Daily, I build up my spirit-man to not fulfill lustful, deceitful enticements. I am the gatekeeper of my eyes and ears. I decide what I allow to enter the window of my soul. I will not be deceived and enticed by the deception of this world that is cloaked as entertainment and other misleading stimuli. It seeks to kill, steal and destroy my destiny, my peace and my joy. Instead, I will meditate on those things that are honest, just, pure and lovely as I refuse to indulge in these deceptive delicacies. Amen.

PSALM 141:4 PROVERBS 23:3 1 CORINTHIANS 15:33
1 JOHN 2:15-16 PHILIPPIANS 4:8

SEPTEMBER 18

Father, I am tired of procrastination robbing me of my time and preventing me from honoring my vows. No longer will I be an accomplice to this thievery. Jesus came so I would have abundant life. Therefore, nothing will rob me of this abundant life. I will do what I need to do to fulfill my purpose and destiny and to glorify you. I know as long as I am connected to you and led by the Holy Spirit, procrastination has taken its last breath. It no longer has control over me. I have taken dominion over it. Thank you for giving me the authority to trample on the serpent's head and to live a life of unparalleled victory! Amen.

ECCLESIASTES 11:4 PROVERBS 6:9-11
JAMES 4:13-14 ECCLESIASTES 9:10 JOHN 9:4
PROVERBS 27:1 ROMANS 7:19-23

19 September

Father, I know sometimes that I become frustrated when my plans are affected by the unexpected. Although I am aware time is in your hands, I often resent that it causes me to alter my schedule. Teach me how to be flexible, as I relinquish my meticulous plans to yours. It is in this state of surrender, the master plan you have set can be accomplished. It is your master plan that catapults me into unimaginable success. It is also in your master plan that I find out who you created me to be, where my faith increases and my character is perfected. Amen.

Psalm 90:12 Psalm 16:11 Jeremiah 29:11
Proverbs 3:5-6 Proverbs 16:9 Proverbs 16:3
Job 23:10 Psalm 18:30 Psalm 37:5
Proverbs 20:24

September 20

Father, You have strategically placed me
on the earth to make a lasting difference.
Bless me to be a ministering agent you can use
in depositing goodness in the lives of others.
Let your miracle-working, transforming power
be manifested in all of our lives. Amen.

Luke 15:10 Psalm 8:4-5
Hebrews 13:1-2 Jeremiah 31:3

21 SEPTEMBER

Father, You have given me an awesome gift of time. Bless me not to squander such a precious gift, but to use it for your glory. Time is the currency in fulfilling my dreams and experiencing an abundant life. Teach me how to use the gift wisely as I make a difference, not only in my life, but the lives of others as well. Show me how to manage my time to fulfill the dreams and desires you placed inside of me. Help me to make this world a better place to live, work, play and worship. Amen.

PSALM 90:12 ECCLESIASTES 9:11
EPHESIANS 5:15-17

September 22

Father, Today I make a commitment to be obedient to all you have instructed me to do. I realize you only want the best for me. When I consult you for guidance, your instruction will always lead me down the path of unparalleled success. Each day, I become more confident in embracing the plans you have for me as I am transformed into all you envisioned before I breathed my first breath. Amen.

Jeremiah 29:11-13
Proverbs 8:33-35   Isaiah 55:8-9, 11
Joshua 1:8   Psalm 1:1-3

23 September

Father, Give me wisdom and courage to speak to the storms in my life with the same authority Jesus did. Give me faith to know I can speak those things that be not, and they will be. In the quiet storms, I will use my time wisely to fortify myself so I can stay focused during the turbulent times as I proceed confidently toward my destiny and purpose. Amen.

1 Kings 5:3-5

Mark 4:37-39

September 24

Father, There is so much that you have for me. Sometimes, I hesitate because of the "what ifs" in my life. This unreasonable preoccupation with what may or may not happen, oftentimes, prevents me from stepping out on faith. I know that no matter what you have said, all I have to do is believe. No longer will I bury my talents and gifts because I am afraid of the "what ifs".

I will conquer them. I know inside of me is a wellspring of talents and gifts, waiting to be unleashed at your command. I not only embrace them, but will use them for your glory, regardless of the "what ifs." Amen.

JUDGES 6:15 PROVERBS 26:13
1 SAMUEL 9:7 JOHN 6:62

25 September

Father, I thank you for your masterful craftsmanship in creating me. Bless me to embrace all you have created me to be and not to listen to what others say about me. As I proceed through the journey of life, reassure me daily of all the wonderful things that you have placed inside of me as I fulfill my dreams and walk in my destiny. Amen.

JEREMIAH 29:11-14A
PROVERBS 8:33-35 PSALM 139:13-18

September 26

Father, Sometimes I don't understand all that is happening in my life. But I'm learning to forget the failures and continue to press toward the prize that you have for me. No longer will I allow the losses in life to consume me. I will view each loss as a dressed-up victory, propelling me into my destiny and my purpose. Amen.

Proverbs 12:14

Proverbs 12:27   1 Corinthians 9:23-25

Philippians 3:13-14

27 SEPTEMBER

Father, Bless me to become all you created
me to be. The plans you have for me are for a
bright future with endless possibilities. As I become
more dedicated to living my dreams and fulfilling
my purpose, I will seek you and know I will find
you. In the process of finding you, I will discover
me. In this self-discovery, I make a commitment
to be dedicated to walk in my destiny as
I fulfill my purpose. Amen.

ACTS 20:24 PHILIPPIANS 1:6
ROMANS 12:1-2 HEBREWS 10:23

September 28

Father, You have placed so many dreams inside of me. Bless me not to be afraid to live every one of them. Provide me with wisdom to know with whom I can and cannot share my dreams. Place the right people in my pathway who will help me fulfill my dreams. Keep me from acting on my dreams prematurely. Enable me to be patient in the process as I team up with you in making all my dreams come true. Amen.

Psalm 14:6

Numbers 12:6

29 September

Father, I realize my very existence is not about natural bread, but living bread. I do not exist by bread alone but by every Word that comes forth out of your mouth. The only way I can overcome the strongholds that prevent me from my destiny and purpose is when I resist the adversary with Your Words, just like your Son Jesus did. Your forcible double-edged Word slashes every negative thing or thought the adversary sends. I overcome by the blood of the Lamb and the forcible words of my testimony that resonate with life and not death. Amen.

JOB 6:25, LUKE 4:1-5, JAMES 4:7,
EPHESIANS 6:12-18, DEUTERONOMY 8:3

SEPTEMBER 30

Father, I am no longer afraid to deal with the emotions that limit me. For too long they have been craftily hidden away causing stagnation and fear. I know that whatever I set my mind to do or become I will achieve it with overwhelming success. Because of my ever-increasing expectation and confidence in You and who You created me to be, I am no longer afraid as I experience the abundant life You envisioned devoid of fear. Amen.

EPHESIANS 3:19-20, JEREMIAH 29:13
PROVERBS 8:35

OCTOBER

Prayer brings on the mind of Christ,
causing you to meditate on positive things
instead of negative ones. It removes you
away from those things that do not build
you up, but pushes you forward toward
those things that increase you
for greatness.

PHILIPPIANS 4:1-8

October 1

Father, I will do whatever it takes to make sure when the clock winds down on this final quarter, I have given it my all in glorifying You! I may not have been as diligent as I should have been, but I will not allow that to prevent me from finishing big. I am more than a conqueror! I am running this race to succeed! Thank You, God! I am a winner! Amen.

1 CORINTHIANS 9:24-27
HEBREWS 12:1-2

2 OCTOBER

Father, We pray for increased funding for research to eradicate breast cancer, so no one will have to suffer from the horrific effects of this debilitating disease. Bless those who actively work to raise funds. Give them favor with donors from every facet of our society. Bless them with strength, endurance, ingenuity, resources and strategies to fulfill their assignment. Amen.

EXODUS 35:29

October 3

Father, We pray for the healing of those suffering from breast cancer and for the strength of those who care for them. Bless them not to become weary in this battle. Give them your supernatural strength, joy and peace to endure, knowing they are victorious. We connect our faith with theirs as we decree and declare they are prospering and in health, even as their souls prosper. Amen.

3 John 1

Isaiah 53:5

4 October

Father, My hands are no longer closed.
I will no longer hoard what's in my hand.
I have been loosed to sow when and where you
say to sow. I am breaking the back of lack and
limitation of my wealth and my mindset toward
wealth. I will no longer be afraid to sow.
I will sow cheerfully, bountifully
and generously. Amen.

2 Corinthians 9:6-7

October 5

Father, Bless me to celebrate those whom I love. Don't let the sun go down on my wrath. Bless me to get over the anger quickly. Don't allow it to fester and grow. Bless me to resolve issues quickly with family and friends so I will have no regrets. Don't allow bitterness to take root. Bless each of us not to allow pride to prevent us from discussing and resolving our differences while continuing to celebrate and love each other. Amen.

EPHESIANS 4:26

6 October

Father, I can only stand on your report that by the stripes of Jesus Christ, I am already healed. I align my faith with your Word. I may not be able to see it in the natural. The report may not be favorable but I am standing on the veracity of your Word that I am already healed. When I feel I can't keep moving, I know you will send someone whose faith will help bolster my faith as I am healed as I go. Amen.

Isaiah 53:5

Luke 17:11-19

October 7

Father, The harvest is plenteous, but the laborers are few. I pray to you, the Lord of the harvest, to begin with me in sending laborers to the harvest field. The harvest is ripe in the missionary field of the marketplace. Amen.

Matthew 9:37-38
Luke 10:2

8 OCTOBER

Father, Thank you for your endless faithfulness. It transcends the linear time of this world and moves into eternity. Whatever you have promised, you are always faithful in delivering within your time. Amen.

HEBREWS 10:23

October 9

Father, I am totally surrendered to your will for your glory. No longer does my will supersede your will. I realize you have strategically positioned me for your glory and your purpose. You have equipped me to excel and achieve greatness. As I go from day-to-day, I go in your will and for your glory. Amen.

1 Corinthians 10:31

1 Peter 4:11

10 OCTOBER

Father, It appears people are waiting and depending on me. I wait and depend on you.

My movement is contingent upon your movements. As others look to me for guidance and direction, I can only look to you for guidance and direction. In the fullness of your time, the waiting will not be just for me. It will be for those who wait and depend on me, as I wait and depend on you. Amen.

Psalm 27:14

Proverbs 3:6

October 11

Father, Thank you for answered prayer. Though the answer may tarry, I will never stop seeking you in prayer until you give me peace in the answer. I unequivocally know that before I prayed, you had already answered and dispatched your angels on my behalf. Amen.

PSALM 27:14

ISAIAH 65:24 PSALM 91:15

12 October

Father, I'm learning how to say, "No," in order for me to bask in your presence for renewal, revival and refreshing. Exercising the power of "No" actually is a "Yes" to you. This enables me to selflessly give of myself with passion and fervency of spirit to you and to others. Amen.

Romans 12:2

October 13

Father, I will dance for you! My feet move in orchestrated precision as I dance for you. I unashamedly, unabashedly dance for you! Oh, how I love dancing in your presence. I am overjoyed! I am excited! I am free to dance and to dance and to dance! With each step, I am empowered! I am set free! I am liberated! I am exuberant! I will dance! Amen.

PSALM 149, 150

14 OCTOBER

Father, Nothing compares to the relationship I have with you. I am in a love affair totally beyond compare. Nothing will ever separate your love for me, and I have no intentions of separating my love from you. It is endless! There is no beginning and no end. It is unconditional! Our love just is! I love you with every ounce of my being—heart, mind, body and soul. Loving you with every ounce of my being still pales in comparison to the breadth and depth of your love for me. Amen.

ROMANS 8:31-39

October 15

Father, Your blessing makes me rich and adds no sorrow with it. The rippling effects of your blessing are far-reaching and propel me into abundance that I never imagined possible. Amen.

Proverbs 10:22

16 OCTOBER

Father, Life is exciting. So much is happening. I'm just basking in the season of elevation and harvest. You are a purposeful God who keeps your promises. It may appear as though you have forgotten, but you are always right on time. Sometimes, it's a struggle and it appears as though I'm being stretched beyond measure. Thank you for entrusting me with these faith-building exercises that take me from glory to glory. Amen.

ROMANS 12:3

2 THESSALONIANS 1:3

October 17

Father, Bless me to be able to confront situations without exacerbating the problem. I may have been offended or offended someone unintentionally, but it has caused a blockage in communication. Establish a time for us to meet and discuss our differences. Bless each of us to be able to talk to each other and not at each other so we can reach a positive amicable resolution. Amen.

MATTHEW 5:23-24

18 October

Father, Teach me to live wise and well. Each day, I will maximize every effort as I exercise wisdom and prudence in everything that I do. I will not allow distractions to prevent me from being productive. I am on a mission to succeed and no one and nothing will detour me from accomplishing what I need to get done each and every day. Amen.

PSALM 90:12

October 19

Father, Thank you for giving me the vision and continually whispering in my spirit not to give up. Thank you for pushing me forward. Although the vision may be delayed, I know that it will happen. I will be diligent in doing what I know to do, praying incessantly, because I know you have already answered the prayer. If you gave me the vision, you have empowered me to fulfill it and your provision is inevitable. Amen.

HABAKKUK 2:1-3

20 October

Father, I am walking into my destiny. I will not faint. I will not get weary. I definitely will not give up. The infamous "they" will not hold me back. I will not allow the pain from calluses and bunions to stop me. If I have to crawl, I will reach my destiny and fulfill my purpose. My determination is encircled with powerful words, augmented with big actionable steps that propel me forward to achieve greatness. Amen.

Isaiah 40:31

Job 6:25

October 21

Father, I thank you for answering my prayers. I may not always agree with your timing or even your answers, but I rest in the dependency of your sovereignty for what is best for me that ultimately guides me to success. Amen.

PROVERBS 3:5-6

22 OCTOBER

Father, As long as I have breath in my body, and I'm in my right mind, I will achieve great feats. The game isn't over until I take my last breath. I will not crawl up into a hole and do nothing. I have set my sights high and I will not settle for less. There is nothing I can't do! I can do all things through Christ who gives me the strength to achieve mighty feats. I am a winner in the game of life! Amen.

PHILIPPIANS 4:13

October 23

Father, You have no respect of persons and you will reward those accordingly by their deeds—good or bad. It is the same with those in authority who do not do the right thing on behalf of the people. You placed them in power and you can remove them. Open their hearts to the cries of the people and their ears to adhere to your wise counsel. Help them to render service with goodwill, knowing you are watching them. Amen.

EPHESIANS 6:9

ACTS 10:34 ROMANS 2:11

24 October

Father, Families are adversely affected by the actions of the government. Programs and services are being decreased and having an adverse effect on the people. Only you can transform the minds and hearts of those in authority to do the right thing so families are able to meet their obligations and live life to its fullest. Amen.

ROMANS 13:1

October 25

Father, Those in authority made the decision not to pay workers, but to continue receiving hefty compensations. Give them a heart of compassion for the people to treat them as they treat themselves. Only you can touch their hearts to set their selfish agendas aside and do the right thing on behalf of the good of the people. Amen.

Romans 13:1

Nehemiah 5:7

26 OCTOBER

Father, I have been redeemed from the
curse of the law from poverty, sickness,
disease and any other maladies of this world.
I am prospering and in health, even as my soul
prospers. I walk in the fullness of your blessing.
You load me up daily with your benefits too
numerous to recant. Amen.

PSALM 68:19

GALATIANS 3:13 3 JOHN 1:2

October 27

Father, You desire us to prosper and be in good health, even as our souls prosper. We pray for the leaders of this country to break through the barriers of division. Bless those you have placed in leadership positions in this country to work together for the good and well-being of the people. Amen.

PSALM 133

28 October

Father, I know that you placed those in authority, not for them to be self-serving, but for them to be servants to the people. We cry out for those in authority, not to place their self-centered wills and agendas over the well-being of the people. Touch their hearts to overcome their divisive-driven behavior for the good of our country. Never let them forget that you allowed them to be in these positions of authority. It was not by their might or power, but you made them servants for the people. Amen.

ZECHARIAH 4:6 NEHEMIAH 5:7
ROMANS 13:1

October 29

Father, Bless me to walk away from toxic relationships. No longer will I associate with people who tolerate and berate me. I will only embrace and establish healthy alliances with individuals who celebrate me. I will no longer allow their toxic words and actions to be catalysts that prevent me from becoming all that you envisioned. Amen.

GALATIANS 5:7-10

30 OCTOBER

Father, I celebrate the sacrifice of
your Son, Jesus Christ, who died on
the cross, bore all of our sins and infirmities,
and gave us a blood-bought covenant right
into an abundant life on earth and eternal life
with you. I am forever grateful. Because of
His selfless act of love and obedience,
I am not bound by the limitations of
this world. I excel in all I do. Amen.

Isaiah 53:3-6

John 10:28

October 31

Father, Thank you for simply being my God. Thank You for loving me so much that you purge and prune me for the Master's use. Amen.

JOHN 15:1-3

NOVEMBER

Prayer catapults you into a place where you move beyond yourself in serving others. You understand that your destiny, purpose and assignment are about people and connected to people always.

EPHESIANS 2:10

November 1

Father, When I look at my hands, all I can see is your favor on them. Because of your favor, everything my hands set out to do is tremendously blessed. Wow! This far exceeds any magic touch. This is the miracle working power of your increased favor and overflowing blessing for my success. Amen.

PSALM 90:17

2 NOVEMBER

Father, I am a warehouse of uncommon seeds of time. Teach me to number my days so I can apply my heart to wisdom. I not only plant seeds for a bright future for me, but for others as well. I sow seeds for spiritual, personal and professional development to reap an abundant harvest. My investment flings open doors of opportunity. Thank you for allowing me to plant seeds in the lives of others so they can become all you created them to be.
I no longer am a time waster,
but a time planter. Amen.

PSALM 90:12

November 3

Father, You are absolutely awesome! I woke up this morning and just wanted to thank you for everything. I may not always understand, but I know that everything is working out for my good. I just want to say, "Thank you," for being the almighty God who never forgets me! There is none other besides you, and I simply love and adore you. Amen.

Psalm 100

4 NOVEMBER

Father, During this season of famine,
help me to stay focused on your sufficiency.
With reports of companies failing, job shortages
and layoffs, I unequivocally know your riches
and glory are meeting my daily needs. I have
plenty because of my dependence on you. Joy,
love and peace well-up from the depths of my
soul and flow outward to others. I release my
confidence and trust in this world's system.
I embrace yours with its abundant
and illimitable possibilities. Amen.

PHILIPPIANS 4:19
PSALM 118:8-9 PSALM 20:7

NOVEMBER 5

Father, In this season of manifestation,
I expect an abundant harvest. You, alone,
are the one who supplies my every need.
Regardless of the size of my expectation,
you are doing exceedingly, abundantly,
more than I could ever ask or imagine possible.
Your super naturalness exceeds my loftiest
expectations of abundance. Amen.

EPHESIANS 3:20

PHILIPPIANS 4:19

6 NOVEMBER

Father, My attitude has much to do with
my success. I need your help. I will no
longer allow outside circumstances to dictate
my attitude. Bless me to understand how my
attitude affects those whom I love and those
who love me. Teach me how to control myself,
especially my temper, so I can make wise decisions
as I seek your advice for direction. Thank you
for guidance in moving confidently
in the plans you have for me. Amen.

EPHESIANS 4:26-27
PROVERBS 29:11 JAMES 1:19-20
ECCLESIASTES 7:9 COLOSSIANS 3:8

November 7

Father, Teach me how to surrender my will to your will. I've been trying to accomplish so much on my own, but I realize I can't do it without you. Actually, I can't do it unless you are the guiding force in my life. I simply need your guidance and direction in every area of my life for me to succeed. Amen.

ROMANS 6:13

8 NOVEMBER

Father, In you I live, move and have
my being. Please show me how to move
according to your plans. Bless me to just do it!
Regardless of the obstacles that I may confront,
guide me safely and swiftly over the hurdles
to success. Teach me, daily, how to complete
the action steps to achieve it as I run this
race of victory. Amen.

1 CHRONICLES 28:20

JAMES 1:5

November 9

Father, Thank you for a transformed mind to expect the impossible because you are the God of impossibilities. I expect you to keep your promises because you are the God of covenant. I hold fast to my profession of faith because I know you are faithful who promised. It is my faith that ensures me that the things I expect, though I may not see them, exist. I am brave! I am strong! I will not give up on expecting you to prosper me as I walk in the abundance of your promises. Amen.

JOB 12:4 JOB 14:14B PSALM 31:24
ISAIAH 54:17B ACTS 26:6

10 November

Father, Chaos can only mean one thing—
you are near. If you weren't, the enemy wouldn't
care. When you are in close proximity, I know
I am going down the right path. I no longer
succumb to familiar deceptions of distraction,
fear, discord and chaos. I have hidden your Word
in my heart and I emulate the example of Jesus.
I hurl your words and slash deceptive tactics
as I proceed down the path of success with
exceeding joy and peace that passes all
understanding. Amen.

PSALM 119:11
PHILIPPIANS 4:7

NOVEMBER 11

Father, You have placed each of us in this world for a purpose. You have placed us in families, businesses, places of worship and communities to work together in harmony to ensure that each of us achieves what you created us to be. Teach me how to be positive, committed and accountable to my family, my church, my friends, my vocation, my community, others and, most importantly, to you. Amen.

PSALM 133

12 November

Father, I envision owning a business. Bless me with wisdom, understanding, counsel, might, knowledge and the revenue needed to start and operate the business. Bring mentors into my life to coach me to become successful in business with integrity and compassion. Bless me to encourage and support the endeavors of other business owners. As my business grows, bless me to be a blessing to others and to treat my employees, vendors, clients and customers as I would like to be treated. Amen.

Isaiah 11:2

Ephesians 6:9

November 13

Father, Thank you for giving me authority to speak into existence things that be not, as though they are. Bless me to maximize my gifts, talents and time wisely and to use wisdom and knowledge as a co-creator in making the world a better place. You are the Master Creator and I am your offspring. Bless, guide and direct me as I strive to emulate your master plan in making this world a better place to live, work, play and worship. Amen.

Psalm 90:12

Proverbs 3:6 Romans 4:17

14 NOVEMBER

Father, You have uniquely created me for greatness. I will not diminish my own self-worth by comparing myself to others. They can never be me, and I cannot be them. I will love others and not be consumed with jealousy and envy. I will use my energies to seek your will for my life. You have fearfully and wonderfully made me. The plans you have for me are good and not evil, with a great future of opportunities. Amen.

GALATIANS 6:4-5
2 CORINTHIANS 10:12 JAMES 3:16

November 15

Father, I will no longer be numb because of the adverse effects of age-old hurts. No longer will they prohibit me from cultivating a relationship with you and others. As I become all you envisioned, I take authority and open my heart, mind and soul to receive your healing in overcoming these hurts. You have great things for me to do, and I will not leave this earth without fulfilling my purpose. Amen.

MATTHEW 18:15
MATTHEW 18:21-22 MARK 11:25-26

16 NOVEMBER

Father, No longer will I allow the derogatory words and actions of others to define me. I pray for them because I realize they dislike themselves more than they dislike me. Heal them of the hurt that causes them to lash out and hurt me and others. Bless them to embrace you so they can learn how to love, not only themselves, but others and you as well. Amen.

JOB 19:2 MATTHEW 12:36-37
2 TIMOTHY 2:16 1 CORINTHIANS 15:33

NOVEMBER 17

Father, I've decided not to allow negative words to be the guiding force in my life. You are the only one who can say what I am and will be. What "they say" no longer has control over my feelings, my emotions and my destiny. It is what, "I AM says," that brings life. It is what, "I AM says," that I will meditate on day and night as you make my way prosperous and I experience great success! Amen.

JOB 19:2 PSALM 52:4
ECCLESIASTES 7:21 MATTHEW 10:28

18 NOVEMBER

Father, I realize people feel the need to say unkind things. Bless me to rise above negative words spoken about me. Don't let me allow them to determine my destiny, causing me not to fulfill my purpose. Bless me to rise above them as I become all you envisioned and experience the abundant life you predestined for me. I also forgive those who feel the need to speak venomous words about me. I ask you to forgive and bless them, as well. Amen.

JOB 19:2 PSALM 52:4
ECCLESIASTES 7:21 MATTHEW 10:28

NOVEMBER 19

Father, At times, going back is necessary. I may not understand why, but I know you will reveal it. I feel like I'm in a comatose state and not living, but merely existing. Your desire is for me to have an abundant life. Regardless of how painful it may be to overcome the effects of my past, I have to go back to where it started. It may appear that I have forgotten, but the lingering residue prevents me from moving forward.

Confronting my past propels me to unimaginable success. Amen.

Exodus 4:20

Genesis 16:9-10 John 11:7-8

20 NOVEMBER

Father, Unforgiveness prevents me from becoming all you envisioned. Right now, I surrender age-old hurts and disappointments. Whether or not they were intentional, I forgive them for what they did to me. I forgive myself for harboring unforgiveness. I ask you to forgive them and me. Thank you for helping me release the bitterness of my past. Now, I can move forward and embrace the abundant blessings you have for me. Amen.

MATTHEW 18:15
MATTHEW 18:21-22 MARK 11:25-26

November 21

Father, Please reveal to me those hurts and disappointments that haunt me and continue to have an adverse effect on my life. I have carried them inside of me so long that I'm not aware of their effect on me. I may feel I have it under control, but I really need your help to forgive those persons who hurt me. Help me release these feelings, once and for all, so I can move forward. Amen.

MATTHEW 18:15

MATTHEW 18:21-22 MARK 11:25-26

22 November

Father, Reveal to me the thing you created me to do. Regardless of the consequences or monetary compensation, I will diligently do it with a spirit of excellence and fervency of spirit. Embolden me to effect change with the same passion exhibited by your Son, Jesus, in fulfilling my destiny and purpose. In fulfillment of my passion-driven assignment, it will enable others to fulfill their divine assignments with purposeful passion. Amen.

ACTS 18:25 JOHN 2:17
ROMANS 12:11 ACTS 1:3

November 23

Father, At times, I need encouragement.
I look around and no one is there, but me.
I need a pep talk. I realize the pep talk can only
come from me. That is when I go deep inside, seek
you, and encourage myself with your words. Your
words spawn a wellspring of life inside of me and
propel me into knowing that I can do all things
through Christ, who strengthens me.
I am unstoppable in achieving all you
purposed for me. Amen.

1 SAMUEL 30:6 PROVERBS 12:25
PSALM 86:7 PSALM 121:1-2
2 CORINTHIANS 1:4
PSALM 37:4 PHILIPPIANS 4:4

24 NOVEMBER

Father, during this Thanksgiving season, I will stop and reflect on all you have done for me. I give you thanks for your omniscience, omnipotence and omnipresence. Sometimes, it seemed a little rough, but I know you have always and will always be with me, leading and guiding my every step. Because I love you so much, and you love me even more, I just wanted to say, "Thank you." Amen.

PROVERBS 3:3-6

PSALM 100 PSALM 107:1

November 25

Father, Sometimes I forget that without you, I am nothing and I would not exist. Regardless of my circumstances, I will seek you daily so I won't lose sight that I have been fearfully and wonderfully created for your purpose. Regardless, if I am in the valley or on the mountaintop, I will exalt and glorify you in all I do. I won't become consumed with my own lack, wants and desires. I won't lose sight of you, the purpose you created me for, and the bright horizon of opportunity you have before me. Amen.

PSALM 131:1-3 PROVERBS 8:34-35
JEREMIAH 45:3-5

26 November

Father, Thank you for the vision and for anointing my hands to write the vision so others can run with passion to its manifestation. I will not be anxious if the vision tarries because I know it will come to pass. Accompanied with the vision is your favor and blessing, with room for massive expansion for illimitable success. Amen.

HABAKKUK 2:1-2

ISAIAH 54:2-3

November 27

Father, Thank you for another day, not to ask for anything, but to just say "Thank you." Every day, you breathe new life into my body. I am so grateful. My situation or circumstances don't matter. I am grateful because you created me with a purpose and, every day, you load me with new benefits and bless me with new mercies. I simply love and adore you. Amen.

LUKE 17:15-16

PSALM 68:19 EPHESIANS 5:20

28 NOVEMBER

Father, Thank you for my family. Thank you for placing inside each of us a commitment to family. Our family is a precious gift that you have given us. It allows us to celebrate our past and revel in our present as we look forward to the future. Each day, we love and celebrate the differences that unite us as one, regardless of age, socio-economic status or individual contributions. Amen.

PSALM 133
EPHESIANS 6:1-4 1 JOHN 1:7

November 29

Father, Thank you for entrusting me to be a conduit of kindness, not just during this season, but throughout the year. I will spread love, joy and peace with everyone who graces my sphere of influence in an expression of gratitude as our lives intersect on this journey called life. Amen.

1 John 4:7-21

30 November

Father, Thank you for creating us to live together in harmony. When that does not happen because of the racial polarization of our society, bring us back to the foundation that each of us has been created in your image. Bless us to celebrate the differences that make us one. Help us to know that no life is more valuable than the next. Bless those who enforce the law to exercise just weights in their actions to all men, regardless of race, creed or color. Amen.

Romans 12:16-18
Colossians 3:12-13   1 Peter 3:8-9

DECEMBER

Prayer opens you to love with every
ounce of your being. It opens you to
live out the greatest two commandments:
to love God with all your heart, mind and
soul; and to love your neighbor as you love
yourself. It allows you the opportunity to
reciprocate the same love God gave to us
when He gave His only begotten
Son that we can live forever.

MARK 12:30-31
JOHN 3:16

1 December

Father, There are times when I may not be inspired to give because I just don't "feel it." Bless me not to abort my abundant harvest by robbing you of tithes and offerings because I am being led by a fleshly feeling as opposed to being spirit-driven. Obedience is better than sacrifice. I will never forsake your instruction to bring all my tithes and offerings to you. I thank you for the fulfillment of your promise to rebuke those things that seek to devour my success and your blessings are overtaking me. Amen.

1 Samuel 15:22
Malachi 3:10-11

DECEMBER 2

Father, I stand at the threshold of a supernatural harvest of uncommon seeds, enabling me to sow into the lives of others. I have great faith that I am a conduit to sow seeds from my abundance into the lives of others so they can sow great seeds of abundance into others' lives. My seeds are my acts, deeds, prayers, words, money and resources. Thank you for an abundant harvest to make an investment in someone else's success and future. Amen.

LUKE 6:38

GALATIANS 6:7

3 DECEMBER

Father, In my limited strength, I cannot do this by myself. I possess great faith and trust in you that you will do exceedingly, abundantly, above all I could ever ask or think, according to the power of your Spirit inside of me. In essence, without you, I am powerless. But with you at the helm, I am more than the entire world against me. I can do all things because you strengthen me daily to be more than a conqueror as I experience unimaginable success. Amen.

EPHESIANS 3:20
ROMANS 8:31 PHILIPPIANS 4:13

December 4

Father, I never want to be so prideful that
I think I have done it all by myself.
My success is not because of anything I have
done, but because of you and your Spirit.
As I reap the harvest of your blessing, I will
seek you for guidance and direction. Please fill
me, daily, with your Holy Spirit so I can function
in the supernatural abundance of your wisdom,
understanding, counsel, might and knowledge
as I give reverence to you for my
daily success. Amen.

ISAIAH 11:2

ZECHARIAH 4:6 1 SAMUEL 30:6

5 December

Father, I want to cry out for others, yet I find myself discussing my own needs and concerns. It is not that I don't care about others, but I need to be strengthened and refreshed. I can't help anyone until I am whole, myself. Bless me not to feel guilty about this time I desperately need to spend with you. Teach me how to embrace this time as being instrumental in my spiritual growth. It is during this time of refreshing and renewing that I am able to envision myself as you do and help others even more. Amen.

MATTHEW 26:36 MATTHEW 26:39
PHILIPPIANS 4:6 LUKE 6:12-13

DECEMBER 6

Father, you placed the ability to succeed inside of me. This has nothing to do with whom I work for as much as it does with the quality of my work. I am an economic entity—Me, Inc.— with the ability to succeed in all I do. Bless me, when my services are no longer needed, to confidently move on to new economically rewarding relationships that need my time, skills and talents. Amen.

PROVERBS 31:13-22, 24-27   PSALM 75:6-7
EPHESIANS 6:7-8   JEREMIAH 29:11   EPHESIANS 4:1
EPHESIANS 4:4   PROVERBS 27:23-24
PROVERBS 22:29   PROVERBS 24:3-4

7 December

Father, Things are changing rapidly and I do not know what to expect. One day, everything seems to be fine and the next, it seems like nothing goes right. I need your guidance. No longer will I be afraid to move confidently forward as I embrace and celebrate the constancy of change. I know you will never leave me nor forsake me. I will be strong and courageous in moving forward as you make my way prosperous and I experience great success. Amen.

1 CHRONICLES 28:20 JOSHUA 1:8-9
PSALM 1:3 ECCLESIASTES 3:1,11

DECEMBER 8

Father, Bless me to open my ears to hear your Word and turn from the cursed things that seek to destroy me. I know your Son, Jesus, came so I can have an abundant life. Open my spiritual eyes to see destructive paths. Provide me with your strength and courage to walk away from those things and people who mean me no good. Joining with you, I am more than victorious in conquering and overcoming these strongholds. Amen.

JOHN 10:10 JOHN 10:5 1 PETER 5:8
GENESIS 19:17-19 DEUTERONOMY 30:19
PROVERBS 14:12

9 December

Father, I will no longer be indecisive.
I will be decisive and make choices that are
pleasing in your sight. As I hide your Word
in my heart, I ask that the Holy Spirit help
me to make God-centered choices that propel
me further into my destiny, fulfilling
my purpose on earth. Amen.

DEUTERONOMY 30:19 REVELATION 3:15-16
ROMANS 8:5-8 MATTHEW 13-14

December 10

Father, I woke up this morning with praises on my lips for your awesome gift of life. You have fearfully and wonderfully created me for stupendous success! I am forever grateful. Your thoughts for my success are innumerable. I will not squander my gift. Every day, I will maximize my gift of life to glorify you in all I do as I become all you envisioned. Amen.

PSALM 139:13-18

11 December

Father, You have placed visions and dreams inside of me. I have been idle long enough and must arise, take responsibility, and do it. I unequivocally know you have provided me with the resources, talent and people I need for success. You gave the vision and I know you are with me as I take ownership and responsibility for the vision and the dream in providing spirit-centered leadership for unparalleled success. Amen.

HABAKKUK 2:1-2

December 12

Father, Bless me to be a person of my word. Regardless if I make a vow to you, others, or myself, I will honor it. As I walk out my integrity, I will honor my commitments and will not waver. It is best not to make a vow than to make one and not honor it. This is especially true of my vows to you. In order to embrace respect for my vows, it begins with honoring my commitment to you, which flows out of honoring my commitments to others and myself. Amen.

DEUTERONOMY 23:21

13 DECEMBER

Father, Thank you for blessing me with a family to celebrate. We may not always agree, but we love each other. You created each of us for greatness and I celebrate the uniqueness of each individual member of my family. I pray for their success. It is because of this uniqueness that we are empowered to celebrate the differences that make us one. Your sovereign will has placed me in this family and, for that, I am grateful. Amen.

PSALM 68:6

PSALM 133

DECEMBER 14

Father, I am experiencing sadness at the thought of celebrating the holidays without my loved one. Sometimes, it's just hard to get up and start my day. The intensity of the grief overwhelms me and it's hard to find joy. I know my loved one is with you, but I miss them. Help me to overcome this grief. You are my comforter. You are my strength. I lay this grief at your feet as you give me beauty for ashes, your oil of joy for mourning and a garment of praise for a heavy spirit. Thank you for turning my mourning into dancing. Amen.

ISAIAH 61:2-3

PSALM 30:11

15 December

Father, My prayers are for those who are experiencing intense grief. Bless them with your beauty for ashes, your oil of joy for mourning and your garment of praise for the spirit of heaviness. Bless them to find peace and joy from the memories of their loved one, as they celebrate this holiday season. Bless me to be a blessing to them with acts of kindness. Bless me to love and to help them through the holidays. Help me bring joy in lifting their spirits. Amen.

ISAIAH 61:2-3
PSALM 30:11

December 16

Father, Happy people make other people happy. I'm so glad you've blessed me with an abundance of happiness to share with others so they can experience an abundance of happiness. Happiness breeds happiness. It is my hope and prayer that those I bestow happiness to will do the same for others as we all experience an abundance of joy. Amen.

2 John 1:12   Isaiah 12:6
Philemon 1:7   Proverbs 15:23

17 December

Father, I embrace the fullness of your joy! This joy supersedes mere happiness. It is an overflowing wellspring of joy that propels me forward, regardless of the circumstances or what's happening in my life. Thank you for your overflowing joy that strengthens and completes me to fulfill my assignment and live out my purpose. Amen.

Psalm 41:1

Isaiah 9:3

December 18

Father, This is the day you have created, and I will rejoice and be exceedingly glad—again, I will rejoice! Weeping may have endured for a night, but your joy has burst forth in the morning. I am breaking out and spreading joy in every place I go and to everyone who comes in my sphere of influence. I am rejoicing forevermore! Amen.

PSALM 118:24 PSALM 30:5
PHILIPPIANS 4:4

19 December

Father, I count it all joy as I go through every trial and tribulation, knowing I am able to endure with passionate patience. This endurance increases my hope that will never make me ashamed because of the overflowing love you have poured in me through your Holy Spirit. Amen.

ROMANS 5:3-5
JAMES 1:2-4

December 20

Father, I delight myself in you as you give me the desires of my heart. You have set a path of continuous success before me. As I meander through the vicissitudes of life, you are forever with me. In your presence is the fullness of joy that strengthens me to endure and to never, ever give up on a path that's paved with success. Amen.

Psalm 16:11

Psalm 37:4

21 DECEMBER

Father, Bless me to be a spark of love, joy and kindness in someone's life. The spark of love, joy and kindness I give to someone else, they will, in turn, give it to others. These sparks will ignite into an endless flame of love, joy and kindness across the world. Amen.

GALATIANS 5:22
JOHN 13:34-35

December 22

Father, There is so much joy here! Even when sadness tries to overtake me, I am overcome with your overwhelming joy. Your joy saturates the very essence of who I am. It is this joy that wells up inside of me with singing and melodies unto you. I will sing and boast of your goodness, your loving-kindness and your tender mercies all the day long. I will rejoice and be exceedingly glad. Again, I will rejoice! Amen.

PSALM 9:2 PSALM 118:24
PSALM 30:5 PHILIPPIANS 4:4

23 December

Father, This is such an awesome time to share the goodness of the birth of your Son, Jesus. Thank you for this indescribable gift you have bestowed on humankind to redeem us as your own. Now we can enjoy an abundant life and spend eternal life with you. Bless us not to squander this time, but to use it wisely. Bless us to share the good news to a hurting world so others can be reconciled to experience an abundant life and have the right to eternal life with you. Amen.

Matthew 28:19

John 3:16

December 24

Father, It is so awesome to celebrate the birth of your Son, Jesus, and the love you have for humankind. You gave your only begotten Son so we could experience an abundant liberated life in the earthly realm and eternal bliss with you. I am forever thankful that I am no longer entangled with the yoke of bondage, but I live a liberated life in Jesus each and every day. Amen.

John 3:16

Galatians 5:1

25 December

Father, I celebrate with the fullness of joy the birth of Jesus and your love. Bless every family to experience this joy in their celebration of the love you bestowed upon us so we can share that same love with our families, our friends and even our foes. Bless us with a merry heart of thanksgiving and praise as we celebrate Christmas, not just today, but every day of the year. Amen.

Isaiah 9:6-7

December 26

Father, I have been so consumed with myself that I lost sight of who you created me to be. You did not create me for my own selfish gain, but to use my gifts and talents for the greater good in serving others. Every day, I realize my purpose exceeds beyond who I am. As you reveal and reconnect me to my purpose and those you have assigned for me to serve, also bless me with your grace and mercy to fulfill the task with passion, commitment and excellence. Amen.

1 Peter 4:8-10

27 December

Father, I feel I am not keeping abreast of the learning curve in our fast-changing society. Because of fear, I have not honed my skills the way I should. I will no longer allow irrational and perceived rational thoughts to prevent me from personal, professional and spiritual growth. I will seek ways to improve and will no longer be poor. I will no longer pass over opportunities repeatedly.

Thank you for anointing me with wisdom, understanding, counsel, might and knowledge to achieve success in every area of my life. Amen.

ECCLESIASTES 10:10 PROVERBS 27:17
PROVERBS 1:5 ISAIAH 11:2 PROVERBS 24:3-4
HOSEA 4:6 PROVERBS 3:13-18

DECEMBER 28

Father, Bless me with your grace and mercy to embrace the new technology and strategies, not just for me to utilize professionally and personally, but to be an influence in your Kingdom. I'm so excited! I am not afraid to embrace new ideas and strategies as doors of opportunities fling open—such as contracts, promotions, strategic alliances, witty inventions, influence, favor and much more. Yes! I am bursting through door after door with confidence and courage. Amen.

PROVERBS 8:12

REVELATIONS 3:8

29 December

Father, My success is being committed to diligently working with fervency on my path to success. I understand success is dressed up in overalls and called hard work. I am not slothful because hard work propels me forward. You have poured into me wisdom, understanding, counsel, might and knowledge in establishing a good work ethic. You are a rewarder of diligence and my diligent efforts make me wealthy. I've put my overalls on and I'm ready to work. Thank you for anointing me with a great work ethic on my path to success. Amen.

ROMANS 12:11

ISAIAH 11:2 PROVERBS 10:4

December 30

Father, My success is linked to what I do each and every day. Teach me to number my days so that I may apply my heart to wisdom. In maximizing each day, I will wisely use your precious gift of time. Teach me how to count the cost by writing down all I hope to accomplish. Help me to commit those ways to you for guidance and instruction. My diligence in my daily routine and seeking your guidance catapults me to be successful in everything I do. Amen.

PSALM 90:12
LUKE 14:28

31 December

Father, It is such a great feeling to know I conquered those habits that have been conquering me. Since I have teamed up with you, I am experiencing success in every area of my life. Every day when I wake up, I thank you for another day of potential to accomplish all you have entrusted to me. I thank you for your grace and mercy, which enables me to overcome every obstacle in my life that previously overwhelmed me. You are absolutely the greatest! Amen.

JOSHUA 1:9 PSALM 68:19
LAMENTATIONS 3:22-23

ABOUT THE AUTHOR

JACQUI A. SHOWERS

Business Encouragement Coach Jacqui Showers provides a collaborative integrated holistic approach to empower, equip and develop spirit-centered leaders and individuals to be effective change agents in an ever-evolving marketplace for purposeful spiritual, professional and personal living. Showers' bold, in-your-face style is not for the faint at heart. She encourages, equips and empowers you to become all God envisioned so you can experience what God S.A.W.W. (Spiritual, Abundance, Wholeness & Wealth).

She is the visionary and founder of JASSAI LLC, JASSAI Publishing, The ME Place Mentor Empowerment Institute, and The Showers Group Ministries. Showers hosts an annual conference, Oh Break Out Empowerment & Leadership Experience, which equips and empowers individuals to seamlessly integrate spirituality with the reality of the marketplace. Showers shares practical empowering, life-transforming principles during her weekly empowerment hour, 11:59 A Minute 'til Midnight Marketplace Prayer Boot Camp. She also distributes a daily Prayer for Success to an extensive email subscriber list and on her social media platforms. Through her writings, Showers has the unique ability to transform basic life experiences into powerful lessons for illimitable success.

A sought-after speaker, Showers provides unboxed coaching for unboxed success through individual consultations, workshops, seminars, webinars, conferences, books, blogs, and e-blasts for personal, spiritual, professional, business, and leadership development. As a Kingdom solutionist and a marketplace leader with substantial experience in management, business development and marketing communications, Showers has provided consultation, strategic oversight, management and leadership to non-profits, government, corporations and small businesses. Showers is an ordained Elder serving at House of Prayer & Praise Ministries and provides leadership for the Intercessory Prayer Ministry and serves on the Ministerial Alliance. She is a graduate from Wayne State University and resides in Detroit, Michigan.

Showers holds dear the love affair she and God share that's totally beyond compare and her commitment to a consecrated life rooted in prayer, fasting and the Word of God.

Twitter @ShowersBlessing, Facebook, LinkedIn, Instagram, Periscope and Pinterest.

Visit **www.theshowersgroupministries.org** and **www.prayersforsuccess.com** to subscribe to her Showers' Blessing Blog.

I DECIDED: Moving from Resolution to Execution

I DECIDED: Moving from Resolution to Execution empowers you to move from merely writing resolutions to executing them. It was birthed from Showers' inability to accomplish her resolutions until she developed an acrostic that propelled her beyond merely writing her resolutions, that she never accomplished, to executing them. These seven principles—Diligence, Excellence, Confidence, Integrity, Discipline, Enthusiasm and Dedication, will do the same for you.

Affirmations for Success: Daily Affirmations for Marketplace Influencers

Words frame our world. Words transform our mindsets. Words are filtered through our eye-gates and ear-gates into our brains and move down to the heart. We are the gatekeepers of our words and our hearts. Out of the heart, the mouth speaks. *Affirmations for Success* provides you daily affirming words igniting you to achieve illimitable success. Each affirmation propels you to experience massive transformation. ***Affirmations for Success'*** self-affirming words are touch stones, when applied every day will transform your mind, environment and relationships to experience the abundant life God envisioned.

www.ingramcontent.com/pod-product-compliance
Lightning Source LLC
Chambersburg PA
CBHW030215170426
43201CB00006B/92